The Nature of Change

Strategies for Using Nature to Channel Change

Sharon Johnston

The Nature of Change: Strategies for using Nature to Channel Change

ISBN: 9780692296271

ISBN: 0692296271

Library of Congress Control Number: 2014915111
Uzima Life, Belmont, NC

The content of this book is intended for general instruction only. Each person's physical,
emotional, and spiritual condition is unique, as are his or her change circumstances. The
instruction in this book is not intended to replace or interrupt the reader's relationship
with a physician or other professional. Please consult your doctor for matters pertaining to
your specific health and diet. The author and publisher specifically disclaim all responsibility for any liability, loss or risk, personal or otherwise, which is incurred as a consequence,
directly or indirectly, of the use and application of any of the contents of this book.

Published by Uzima Life

Printed in the United States of America

This book is dedicated to my father, who gave me roots into the earth, my mother, who gave me wings to soar to new heights, and my husband who gave me the courage to light a fire with my life.

Contents

Preface

I appear to have always had a restless nature. I started exploring at the age of 15 months when I set out from our home down the dirt road to see where it led. I was discovered three houses down the road. Much to my mother's dismay, that was not the extent of my wandering, as I set out a few months later with my handbag on my arm to see what was up the road the other way. To my pleasure I found a patch of dirt where I played quite happily until I was retrieved.

I spent most of my childhood barefoot, running wild and getting dirty. I loved exploring the forests, biking trails, kayaking across the lake, sailing and camping. I inherited my nature from my father who was always seeking out natural wonders hidden in the ordinary. An undiscovered waterfall in a neighborhood forest, a fossil in a piece of shale, a cosmic event in the sky.

In the winters we would head to the Drakensberg Mountains where we hiked almost all of the trails. At 11 years old I hiked the Sentinel Trail and climbed chain ladders to the top of the Amphitheater at 9600ft. In those days we had no fancy equipment - just a repurposed water bottle on a braided strap. On one occasion I remember we ran out of water and my father's solution was to filter water from a stagnant pond through a handkerchief. We hiked all day and stayed overnight in rustic huts. My grandparents lived near the sea so during school holidays we were at the beach walking for miles in search of the best seashell finds. In those days the beaches were littered with them, though we loved to dash into the surf to find the elusive ones hidden in the trough where the wave curled back on itself. We were also boogie boarders riding the angry surf that is a feature of the South African coast. It was the best childhood I could ever have asked for.

I grew up surrounded by animals, though we only ever purchased one cat. The horses, dogs, birds, rabbits and cats were all given to us. We even had a hamster arrive at the doorstep one day – who knows from where, but he too was given a home. I have always had a need to connect with nature. I remember crying when my parents wouldn't let me take home a mouse I found in the sea dunes. And was ecstatic when I was able to hand-rear a swallow to adulthood and release it into the wild. We still saw that swallow return each year – it stood out as it was a different species to the flock it joined in the area of our home where we released it.

The movie I found most memorable as a child was Born Free. I dreamed of living with the lions.

I worked as a magazine editor and travel writer, visiting Botswana, Zambia, Zimbabwe, Mozambique and other regions of South Africa. After a very intense experience in nature, I realized I really wanted to be an environmentalist however I was talked out of that, much to my later regret. I wrote these words at that time for an article for the magazine.

There is nothing that quite comes close to matching the incredible energy experienced when visiting Africa. It radiates from every pore; you become aware of it in the big skies above you, the earth throbs beneath you to an ancient pulse and you can feel that the people, animals and plants all vibrate with a harmony which is lost to over-commercialized first world metropolises.

It surprises me that I was so clued in to the dynamic of universal energy. It ignited a spark in me that led to me traveling to London and eventually to America in search of something, though I couldn't name what. I felt a burning passion to do something meaningful. Ironically, the catalyst was an illness I was infected with as a child as I played in the hay in the horse stables. I was bitten by two ticks and was infected with rickettsia, a bacterial tick-borne illness that I suspect caused complications as from that point on, I was always struggling with health issues. The chaotic state of my body and immune system only became clear when I was bitten by another tick on a backpacking trip 30 years later and my whole body collapsed due to what I later learned was Lyme disease. Losing my ability to function was extreme and took away 4 years of my life. But it was an entirely good thing as I learned to heal my body and was projected into finding what I really wanted to do with my life. I returned to my first love: nature. I wrote this book *The Nature of Change*, to describe my change cycle of rediscovering my true natural path, and to lay out a guide for others to follow should it so inspire them.

❧❧

I always suspected that what I was struggling with was not normal, as I observed how others sailed through life with ideal health and a never-ending supply of energy and confidence. I never questioned my burden, instead I developed a fighting spirit that enabled me to keep pushing to prove I was able to achieve, regardless of what was thrown at me. I resolved that life was not going to break me. Every time it tried, I channeled the negative energy into fuel to drive me higher and further.

Balanced with the burden, was the blessing of insight. I never realized until a few years ago, that not everyone is born with the ability to read their own energy and signals from their body, read other's energy and feel the dynamic of the earth's energy. I assumed everyone had that ability and I suddenly was struck by the realization that if you are not able to do this, life can be very difficult to navigate. Instinctively knowing the right path to take does not come easy, and so relying on the social messages and cues becomes the only way to identify the commonly accepted path. While in denial of my wild self and my intuition, I used the material blueprint as my guide, and it almost destroyed me, both physically and emotionally.

For most people that one-size-fits-all model is very destructive to their soul, whether they realize it or not. It is even more so if you are a highly sensitive person as you already know you are different so you try harder to fit in, which makes you vulnerable to being controlled or becoming depressed. I saw this first-hand with a friend who was desperately seeking a way out of her hole of addiction, depression, insomnia, food disorders and health crises. It opened my eyes to the world that exists under the cover of the social face that we all wear. We pretend everything is perfect while quietly dying inside. Sadly my friend died at a young age. Her passing ignited in me a desire to understand why the delicate balance of our bodies is disrupted causing unhappiness and ill-health. While I had struggled with my health and life, I had always managed to stay positive, and I wondered if I could capture the philosophy that had sustained me in a simple guide for others to use. As I started writing, all the myriad pieces of my approach to life magically came together into what you are about to read.

I unintentionally became an expert at change having learned the ropes in the school of life as I searched for meaning and purpose in my spiritual evolution. I built successful careers from scratch three times in three countries, and experienced more changes in my health than I can count. It was a natural progression for me to therefore become an expert in change in my job too. I spent twelve years in the corporate arena leading projects that required a change in behavior. After reviewing how projects were implemented and then failed due to the mindset at the time of "build it and they will come", I established that the missing link was the ability of people to adjust to change. I became a Certified Change Manager, and began applying the principles to my projects. When I shifted the focus from the requirements of the systems being designed to the needs of the people using them, I was able to break down the resistance. I engaged people in owning accountability for the change by making it simple and real for them; then empowered them through training and coaching.

Once I had my health crisis and discovered what an absolute mess my body was in, I became determined to learn what one needs to be healthy, and studied to be an Integrative Health Coach. As with all the twists and turns of our universal destiny, these two crises in my life were the catalyst for my movement to the next stage in my change journey. It prompted me to realize the value of using my change management experience, love of nature, and health knowledge to craft a natural strategy for living.

When I examined my own journey through change it became clear that conscious change can be managed through 1. Developing an honest understanding of where you find yourself, where you want to go and why you want to change and 2. Employing nature's strategies to evolve back to a place of harmony with one's mind, body and soul.

In the course of my life I felt drawn to study ancient spiritual knowledge that offers us clues to our true role in the universe. This wealth of knowledge refined my understanding of how to live in harmony with nature, our body and other people. *The Nature of Change* is designed to be a guide that connects the dots of ancient knowledge, with simple strategies for wellness, into an easy to consume roadmap to health and happiness. It provides insight on how to rediscover that instinct that was lost to us by using the best teacher of all, nature. It is a triple thread of soul, mind and body work that is woven together into a spiral that grows and expands as the level of consciousness develops through the change journey.

Each chapter within a stage contains a set of principles that helps to establish the right mindset before embarking on the change strategies to progress through that particular change. There are only five change strategies in each chapter to ensure that the message remains simple and achievable. Each chapter builds upon the prior one to cohesively strengthen your comfort and courage so that you can progress through the continuum of challenges.

I therefore offer you *The Nature of Change* with a humble mission to ignite a movement of enlightened souls who reject unhealthy, unnatural living, and embrace natural change as a growth engine towards a life of harmony within oneself, one's community and our world.

Are you ready to become a Change Maker? Your journey starts now.

The best remedy for those who are afraid, lonely or unhappy is to go outside, somewhere where they can be quite alone with the heavens, nature and God. Because only then does one feel that all is as it should be and that God wishes to see people happy, amidst the simple beauty of nature. As long as this exists, and it certainly always will, I know that then there will always be comfort for every sorrow, whatever the circumstances may be. And I firmly believe that nature brings solace in all troubles.
—Anne Frank, *The Diary of a Young Girl*

Introduction

wild
- living in a state of nature and not ordinarily tame or domesticated
- not subject to restraint or regulation
- passionately eager or enthusiastic
- going beyond normal or conventional bounds
- deviating from the intended or expected course
- indicative of strong passion, desire, or emotion

(Source: Merriam-Webster)

tame
- reduced from a state of native wildness
- not exciting, adventurous, or controversial
- made docile and submissive
- crushed, subdued, depressed
- lacking spirit, zest, and the capacity to excite
- make less powerful and easier to control

(Sources: Merriam-Webster, Oxford Dictionaries, Babylon)

Which word describes your life? Which life would you rather be living? Did you create your life, or was it created for you?

A wild life is a life in which you are in tune with your own inner drumbeat, a life where you feel the rhythms of energy, where the norms of society don't constrict your need and desire to live in harmony with your inner wild child.

A wild one is a person who truly knows him- or herself at an intimate level, who knows and feels the earth's desires and needs because they reflect his or her own. A wild person is so in tune with nature that it is hard to know where he or she ends and nature starts. Speaking with animals is as natural as speaking with a friend. Losing an animal or forest is like losing a family member. Living equally with all creatures on the earth, including trees and other plants, is intrinsic and instinctual.

A wild one is part of a large family of living beings, all of whom follow their instincts. Every species is different and has its own set of unique patterns of behavior that guide its migrations. People have their own guidance system, just like the birds who migrate or the turtles who return to the place of their own birth to nest. Unfortunately we have lost our innate ability to follow these naturally occurring instincts. We have succumbed to a societal pressure that requires all human beings to conform to a prescribed order of living, as laid down by the highest human power.

But what sets human powers as greater than the powers of the universe? The dynamic of the universe should be the ultimate guiding force, and that is personal for each person. Each of us has a journey that is laid out for us. The challenge is that there is no ready-made map or directions. The ability to travel this journey is not a given right. It is an earned one. Living a life in harmony and authenticity holds the key to unraveling the clues to your own life path and ultimately sets you on the path to enlightenment.

The path is not easy. It is full of challenges and barriers to make you question whether you are heading in the right direction. You will be confronted by people who will try to deter you from what they view as your deviation from the norm. Events will happen that will make you question all that is fair and just. Your inner saboteur will attempt to make you doubt your instincts. These are all part of the process of evolution.

Ultimately, the way-finder that helps you navigate these setbacks is your intuition. Developing and trusting your intuition will be your saving grace. This inner guide will help you accept that, on the journey, you will experience trial and tribulation as you earn your levels of enlightenment toward your natural state of being—the state to which you were born and the state to which you need to return if you want to live a life of harmony and peace.

Adopting a wild approach requires you to rethink how you view what happens to you in life, to shift how you perceive events, how you interact with people, and how you feel about nature. Living as a wild one challenges you to change your view of who you are and what your role in life is. We are going to deconstruct what society has carefully crafted as the perfect life and reconstruct it into what the universe deems the *natural life.* Your eyes will be opened to how the "perfect" yet unnatural life has interrupted the life-nurturing flow of energy that every being needs to sustain itself and keep growing. This energy is as important to us as water and sunshine is to a plant. It is our life force. *Chi. Ojas.* It is the source of happiness, harmony, and zestful living.

> *Materialism: a tendency to consider material possessions and physical comfort as more important than spiritual values*

Reconnecting with your life force is the secret to finding a state of bliss that is not driven by how much money you have, how high up the ladder you have climbed, or how many social media friends you have. It is a bliss that is content with a simple life; that values morals above social status, that finds joy in the everyday, and that sees love in everyone and everything.

This book is therefore a life map to help you understand what living wild is about and how to live a life of wildness and wellness. It is not an easy journey. I am going to ask you to set aside your entrenched beliefs and your preordained behaviors and ask you to embrace a more free-form, instinctual way of living.

I am going to ask you to accept and embrace the law of change that states that you will keep repeating the same mistakes until you realize that you need to change. The natural cycle of change requires you to own the knowledge that not changing is working against the natural order of nature. All of nature changes; human beings also need to change in order to stay in harmony with the universe.

Change is a way of demonstrating your belief between right and wrong, good and bad. Change forces you to take the steps to affirm that you are not going to stay in the same cycle but will break out of the rut. It requires you to demonstrate faith that, while you may not know how the change is going to play out, you are willing to take the steps necessary to move in the right direction.

To make it really simple, I have defined each strategy in terms of only five changes you need to make to achieve that step. These are not complex changes, but breaking the strategy down into five simple changes makes it more manageable and easier to achieve. The benefits of the change are huge, and as you work through the whole program, you will start to see the results and get in tune with your wildly well self.

This book is intended as a guide to rediscovering what you believe is important in life. It is a simple yet direct set of principles that break through all the artifice and lay bare the facts about what is real and what is fake. In each chapter, I describe the principles relating to the stage. Read them, print them, put them on the fridge, and meditate on them. But before you start the strategies for that step, decide that these principles are ones that you believe in, will argue about with someone who disagrees with them, and are willing to go forth and implement as a change proponent, promoting these values as fact. If you can say that these are true statements, then you are ready to start the change strategies.

So often, people start trying to change without having figured out the root of their beliefs. If you can't live, breathe, and sleep a belief, then you will never adopt it. The greatest challenge of change is that you can't do it half-heartedly. It is the whole 150 percent or nothing. That is the honest truth.

If you attempt to make a change when you are only 50 or 75 percent engaged, you will find it easy to succumb to your own inner resistance, which will attempt to derail you. Your roots have to be strong enough to resist the winds of family-ingrained habits, self-sabotage, friend pressure, work dictates, and other destructive forces that try to erode your faith in your beliefs.

Your roots have to be firmly embedded in the grounds of principles. Principles are what set moral behavior. Morals are what create discipline. Discipline is what sets habits. And habits create change.

> *"Plant a thought and you will reap a deed, plant a deed and you will reap a habit, plant a habit and you will reap a character, plant a character and you will reap a fate."*
> —Indian proverb

What I set out to do is explain why these principles should be important to you, in that they allow you to overturn habits that hurt, not just yourself, but the whole survival of our earth. While we may not feel like we need to change, change is a fact of nature; it will happen and not necessarily in a positive way. The longer we resist change, the more we are putting pressure on nature to change. And nature is more than willing and able to change, as demonstrated by floods that have destroyed the earth, blazing meteorites that obliterated the dinosaur life, and freezing ice ages that wiped out all but the hardiest. Everything is interconnected—yin and yang, positive and negative, good and bad. If the balance goes and the overall earth energy sways toward the negative, then that is the course that we are setting for ourselves. And once it gains momentum, there will be no stopping it. We may believe we can control nature, but time and again, it demonstrates that it is our master. We have been given the choice of living in harmony with nature, but consistently, we choose the convenience of living against nature. And that choice will cost us.

The reward for choosing an authentic, natural life is the development of a wellspring of harmony, wholeness, and abundance that overflows into your life. In Africa, where I was born, there is a word in the Kiswahili language that describes a healthy, happy, abundant, energetic life. That word is *Uzima*. It means full of life in all aspects, as there are not multiple words to describe what it means to be living life well. To truly be living, you have to be whole. If any one piece of your existence is out of balance, the rest will be too. The ultimate goal of this book, therefore, is to enable you to reconnect with your natural state of being and feeling, to help you build a whole and healthy life that is totally in tune with your inner self, and to create a life so full of abundance that you marvel every day at the miracle that your life truly is.

Consider a tree for a moment. As beautiful as trees are to look at, we don't see what goes on underground—as they grow roots. Trees must develop deep roots in order to grow strong and produce their beauty. But we don't see the roots. We just see and enjoy the beauty. In much the same way, what goes on inside of us is like the roots of a tree.

—Joyce Meyer

Stage 1 of Change

The Seed

For personal change to be effective, you have to be very grounded in who you are. This requires turning inward and taking a good, hard look under the covers of your life at your values, your health, and your body. Ask yourself if you held a mirror up to your life, would you be completely happy with what you saw? Do you even have the courage to hold that mirror up? Or would you rather keep hiding your truth from even yourself?

I was an old soul from a family of intuitive women. Sadly though, all the women in our family learned ways to shut down our sensitive sides because the gift of being highly sensitive was overwhelming, as you feel the emotions and thoughts of everyone around you. Feeling different is never easy, and as a result, I buried myself in nature and books, becoming somewhat of an introvert. When I did connect up with friends or in relationships, I learned how to please those around me, and as a result, I never had a real sense of self. Learning to be okay with being quirky and different was very difficult for me.

Change takes great courage and intense honesty.

Repeat after me: "I love my true self."

Nobody is bad or flawed at heart. We all start out pure and innocent, and then life comes along and starts writing all over that clean white page. If you're lucky, it leaves happy, uplifting messages that allow you to float in a sea of cotton wool through childhood. But for most people, it is a mix of good and bad that instills a large dose of reality at an early age. We don't recognize that it is okay to be different, that our quirkiness is what sets us apart with our own unique set of gifts and talents. We allow others to infringe on our sense of self, and then we lose sight of who we really are and start modeling ourselves on others in the hope of creating a new reality that way.

Then for some, the messages are brutal, innocence-destroying infringements on their right to view the world through rose-tinted glasses. Learning to trust others is a challenge, and the free spirit is shut down before it has time to fully grow.

Regardless of your starting point, we all have a wild child living in our soul who desires to find his or her way back to a place of contentment, peace, joy, and fulfillment. The journey to finding your wild one starts by identifying and acknowledging what stands in the way on your path. Only then can you start hacking your way through the brambles and overgrowth that is cluttering the way.

A book on wildness would not be complete without touching on what happens when your true nature is repressed. If you keep ignoring that panicky feeling that your life is not happening the way your inner voice knows it should, it will take its revenge on you by finding dark avenues to release its pent-up frustration.

Here is a test for you. When you drink more alcohol than you should, do you start behaving in inappropriate ways? Do you get sexually promiscuous, unreasonably angry or rebellious, or do or say stupid things you know you will regret in the morning? Everyone does this to some degree in the rebellious phase of life between child and adult, but for those in a state of deep-seated wild repression, these behaviors take on extreme forms. It becomes a form of hidden identity that is only allowed out to play when the sweet caress of alcohol woos it from the hidden depths of the soul.

Or do you eat more sugar or candy than you should? You know that it is your master and is controlling you, yet you can't stop feeding the hunger within.

Do you spend more money than you know you should? Is compulsive shopping one of your favorite pastimes? You can't stop going to the mall to engage in mindless shopping for things you don't need but give you a short euphoric feeling and then leave you feeling empty until you get your next retail high.

Do you eat more junk food than you should? You try to resist, but your body demands a hamburger, fries, and a milk shake to fill the craving for comfort food. And you almost feel like you can't stop yourself, even though you tell yourself that this is the last time you give in to the fast-food fix.

Do you obsess about your looks and spend hours working toward creating a perfectly made-up face and well-toned body? Do you freak out if your hair is a mess? Would you never allow yourself to be seen without makeup?

Do you allow someone else to control you? To treat you however they want, abuse your trust, body and emotions to serve their own needs?

If you answered yes to any of these questions, it is a clear message you are not in tune with your wild self.

"To change, a person must face the dragon of his appetites with another dragon, the life-energy of the soul."
—Rumi

The pattern of bad behavior will continue until you are able to face the truth that something or someone (including possibly yourself) is suppressing your true nature in favor of a path society laid out for you. If you don't make a conscious choice to change, typically, the change cycle starts with a crisis that forces you to reevaluate how you are living your life. Maybe you have a health scare or you lose your job. This is the universe at work. All that soul energy that you are repressing will eventually bring you down by force.

At that stage, you will have no choice but to finally listen to what your wild self has been screaming at you in vain and make a complete 180-degree shift in your life to rehabilitate your poor, broken body, mind, and soul.

> *"Change your opinions, keep to your principles;*
> *change your leaves, keep intact your roots."*
> —Victor Hugo

Alternately, you can admit to yourself that change needs to happen. You can make the choice to embark on a quest to find your authentic self. I hope, as you are reading this book, you have already made this decision. This journey will involve a fair amount of introspection and learning about yourself so that you can unlock the gates that are holding your wild nature in check.

When I was in my mid-twenties, I recognized that something was misaligned in how I was living my life. I could not understand what it was, and repressing my intuition led to a period of incredible restlessness within me. This was my stage of desperate running from the truth while paradoxically searching for the answer by constantly shifting. I left my family and roots in South Africa, gave up a great job, and moved to London to experience life in a different place. I was seeking something, but I didn't know what. I still didn't find it in London, so I kept wandering and ended up in America. Yet, still, I couldn't escape my burden of discontent.

I was a terribly lost soul (even though I didn't know it or appear like I was), who relied on codependency to fill the gap of not having my own sense of self. I relied on my ex-husband to guide my life but was very angry inside for being in that role. My only defining attribute was my career, and when I found myself without a job when I first arrived in Florida, I became even more adrift. I started delving into my dark side because there was such a void in my life that it took great extremes for me to feel alive. The problem was I was looking in the wrong places, and I ended up feeling worse about myself.

Here is how my average day would go. I'd wake up, eat a super-unhealthy breakfast, and lounge around in my pajamas for a couple of hours. Then a friend would fetch me (I didn't have a car), and we'd indulge in retail therapy, aimlessly soaking up the glorious negative energy of the mall. Later we'd pop open a bottle of wine, and eat more unhealthy food for dinner. And because I was bored with not having a job, I also got hooked on flirtation, loving the attention misbehaving brought me.

To some, this may feel like the definition they know of *wild*. I was having fun, and doing whatever I pleased—except there was nothing natural about how I was living. In fact, I had descended to a level of self-destruction and was wildly out of control. The harder I tried to feed the quiet desperation, the deeper I spiraled into a dark place in my soul.

> *"The mass of men lead lives of quiet desperation."*
> —Henry David Thoreau

It all came to a head one night when all the repressed feelings just started barreling out of me. I screamed at my husband, and anger I didn't even know was inside me rained down on his head. The next day, I started with chest pains and numbness down my arm. The ambulance came and whisked me to the emergency room, and I got a serious wake-up call. Turns out the stress caused the symptoms. That was when I knew that change had to happen.

I eventually realized that repressing your true nature triggers these addictions or temptations that lead you in directions you have no real desire to go in but that take the edge off the unrequited hunger you feel and blunt the pain of a lost soul.

It was only when I understood that I was living as an orphan from my natural self, reliant on others to provide for me, that I was able to recognize my codependency. Facing my codependency opened the door for me to realize that I had to stand on my own two feet and wasn't being fair to myself or my ex-husband by not figuring out who I was and what I wanted.

Leaving my marriage was one of the hardest things I have ever done, but it was the catalyst for a change toward my wildly natural (as opposed to unnatural) self that was long overdue.

This was my first cycle of change.

⤳ ⤖

This stage of the change journey is therefore about seeking knowledge about yourself and the larger dynamic of the universe, to give you a strong foundation to build your vision on. It is about being honest about the fact that the risk of staying the same is greater than the risk of changing. It requires you to start reconnecting with the natural forces that will be your guides as you shift into your more natural being.

Know yourself and you know the universe.
—Socrates

one

Rediscover Your Authentic Self

The very first question you have to ask is: "Do I know who I am?"

"Yes," you may say, "I know who I am. I am Sharon Johnston, five-two, 120 pounds, blond hair, blue eyes. I was born in South Africa and now live in Charlotte. Isn't that who I am?"

That is the wrapper of who you are. Those are the demographics that are used to describe your identity. They are useful for driver's licenses and passports, social media accounts, and doctors' records, but they are not the full picture of what makes up you.

Our journey through this book is to help you truly find your way back to your wild and natural self. If you ask most people, they honestly don't know. They have their social identity well defined. Some go to great extremes to polish that external self so that it is a glossy package that advertises their best traits well. But dig a little deeper and you will find that most people have completely lost sight of who they are underneath that wrapper. They were taught growing up that the wrapper was most important. The wrapper of success and polish would get them ahead in life, and all else was of lesser consequence, as aren't money and looks all that society values? In the pursuit of that magic wrapper, we are taught that money is the path that leads to the look that everyone will envy and want—the large house, the shiny new car with the right badge, and the clothes that define the size of our bank account.

We believe that when we follow the "green" brick road (as opposed to the yellow), we will arrive at the place where happiness resides and all will be in balance in our life.

Except that is all a crock. And, no, there is no gold in that crock.

Knox College psychology professor Tim Kasser shows, through a series of experiments spanning from six months to twelve years, that when people become more materialistic, their emotional well-being takes a dive.

We were sold a lie and manipulated into an artificial world of stuff, stuff, and more stuff and tied to jobs to pay for that stuff. In the process, we lost sight of who we really are underneath it all. What are our values? What are our soul desires? What is our body telling us? What stimulation do we need that doesn't come from a screen? If you know the answers to these questions, you are lucky, as most people don't.

So where do we start to unravel this mess?

We need to think about ourselves as three separate yet interlinked personalities or identities:

Body Personality
Mind Personality
Soul Personality

Think of each of these as circles that overlap, and where they meet in the middle is the essence of who you are. This is your life force and energy, and it is completely unique to you. If any of our personalities is out of balance or has been abused in any way, it can cause an imbalance in all three. When we work to understand what caused the upset in each circle of our life, we work toward creating a healing balance and finding our wild one, who is in harmony with his- or herself and with the natural world.

Each and every one of us is a hero on a journey called life. This journey has no map or directions. The only guides you are given are your three personalities. You have your brain to strategize the right way, your soul to intuit whether that is indeed the right choice for you, and your body to take you down that path.

If only it were that simple! The universe that manifests in you during this journey we call life has no desire to make things easy on you. You have to earn the right to enlightenment. And this has nothing to do with whether you are a good or bad person, lucky or unlucky, wealthy or poor, educated or uneducated. What it has everything to do with is your desire and ability to recognize the larger order of things, to be aware that, while your ego tries to convince you that you are your own universe, you are the only thing that matters, and all else is of lesser importance, this is a diversion that is created to steer you away from the truth. We are all connected. Everything we do feeds into the universe and builds a virtual energy store that can be a positive or negative balance, depending on how we choose to live our lives. Many of the secrets of the universe are contained in ancient religious texts where the principles of natural living are laid out, the pursuit of godliness is described, and the diversion tactics of temptation are detailed. The principles have been around for thousands of years and yet have become lost to us. Buddhists, Hindus, and early Christians all understood this.

Where organized religion has muddied the waters is by creating a collective consciousness that allows the individual to worship the religion and not the essential source of all things godly: nature. If you strip away the religion wrapper and follow the basic principles for kind and conscious living that every single religious group has, you will start to build your awareness of how the universe truly functions, how *we* are nature. We are God. We are the universe. And our purpose on earth in this journey called life is to shift our consciousness, our way of living, to be in alignment with all other entities that make up this spiritual whole— animals, plants, the air, the sun, the earth. All these things are energetic beings that can nurture and sustain us—or destroy us.

I am not telling you to abandon your religion, whatever it is. I am saying, take a slightly different view and align your religious beliefs with nature. View a forest as your church, a canyon as a cathedral, a tree as your friend, and your pets as able to communicate. See the earth and everything in it as alive and an extension of yourself. If the trees die, we die. If the waters get polluted, we die. If the air gets polluted, we die. If the honey bee dies, we die.

This is the reality. This is what is real and tangible, even though it may seem foreign and intangible to you right now. It is right in front of us. And yet most people can't see the dynamism that keeps all things functioning and that we are inextricably linked.

Learning to "see" this interconnection is how we find our authentic self. The Hindu phrase *Namaste* means "I see you," as does the Zulu greeting *Sawubona*.

> *I honor the place in you where Spirit lives*
> *I honor the place in you which is*
> *of Love, of Truth, of Light, of Peace,*
> *when you are in that place in you,*
> *and I am in that place in me,*
> *then we are One.*
> —Sanskrit blessing

A Zulu folk saying describes this as, "Umuntu ngumuntu naga-bantu," meaning, "A person is a person because of other people."

This isn't seeing with our eyes. This is the third sight, the insight, seeing "in" and not "out," seeing inside others and inside ourselves, seeing the signals our body is giving us, seeing the pain others are suffering, seeing the tremendous pressure the earth is under, and seeing the role that we have to play in change. As you start this journey to reconnect with your wildly authentic self, you will begin to develop this sight. As your awareness and knowledge builds, it will become as easy to use as any of your other senses.

This is the largest secret to change. People who have developed this ability are able to do more, go further, and fly higher. They are not reacting to things after they happen; they are feeling things as they happen. Their intuition and awareness of the energy at play give them foresight of events, and as they unfold, they guide them into making the right choices.

Some people are born with this ability. We call them "old souls" because they have carried this awareness and knowledge with them through the realms of time and space. They are highly sensitive from a young age, and it often overwhelms them, causing them to retreat and become shy or introverted. The Hindu religion defines three basic principles of the universe, known as the gunas: *sattva* (purity and knowledge), *raja* (action and passion), and *tama* (ignorance and inertia). These principles are intangible and are not physical in nature. According to the Spiritual Research Foundation, these three basic components can only be perceived by the subtle sense organs, or our sixth sense (ESP). They describe these as follows:

- The basic *sattva* component is the subtlest or most intangible of the three subtle basic components. It is the component nearest to divinity. Hence, its predominance in a person is characterized by happiness, contentment, and virtues like patience, perseverance, the ability to forgive, and spiritual yearning.
- The basic *tama* component is the basest of the three. Its predominance in a person is reflected by laziness, greed, and attachment to worldly matters.
- The basic *raja* component provides fuel to the other two— i.e., it brings about the action. So depending on whether a person is predominantly *sāttvik* or *tāmasik*, the subtle basic *raja* component will bring about actions pertaining to *sattva* or *tama*.

Everyone has elements of each, but the percentage of each component determines which style of personality dominates. The soul, which is the God within us, is separate from these three components. As we move further toward enlightenment, the influence these elements have on our personalities weakens. People with a strong sense of intuition can pick up the predominant personality in others.

These dimensions also have an influence in the larger universe. If there is an increase in tama or raja in the world, there is an increase in war, terrorist activities, and natural disasters. After a long sattvic history, we are currently in a period of increased tama, and spiritual leaders predict a universal shift to correct the imbalance is coming.

We are therefore challenged to embrace our spirituality and align with the natural order of the universe to redress the balance from the materialistic, egotistic, and negative environment that currently exists on earth.

In his book *Second Wave Spirituality: Passion for Peace, Passion for Justice*, Chris Saade sums it up as follows:

> You and I are part of one of the greatest evolutionary leaps of consciousness. We are witnessing love erupting into global action. We are participating in a worldwide movement of engaged spirituality.
>
> What is required from us is the courage to open our hearts, unleash our love, expand our imagination, and uphold justice in the circles of our life.
>
> The emerging wave of engaged spirituality that we are witnessing is a grassroots phenomenon. Each of us is essential to its maturation and realization. (Preface, xix)

The bottom line is that the time to change and be change is now. Be the hero in your and the earth's story, and join the natural change movement that is growing and blossoming.

Wild Self Principles

I have no desire to be perfect but rather wish to
be authentic to my wild soul's purpose.

I will not fear looking at my flaws and accepting
them as a part of my hero's battle scars.

I view change as an adventure that comes
with challenges and triumphs.

I accept that I am the master of my own journey and destiny.

I respect and love all natural entities on earth
as part of my own family and will adopt a set of
values that are kind to myself and all others.

Your Change Strategy

Step 1: Know where you are in life.

Firstly, it is important to identify what changes you need to make.

Be completely honest, as holding a mirror up to where you are currently, is critical to the change process. Write down what you wish to change.

Step 2: Know who you are.

Make a list of what your passions are. Ask friends and family to share with you what your strengths and weaknesses are. Ask them to be brutally honest, and don't resent them for their honesty.

The journey of life brings out different sides to ourselves, which were defined by Jung as archetypes. Knowing what themes are present in our life at this time, when we are contemplating change, is key to learning to leverage the strengths to push forward and counteract the weaknesses that may hold us back.

Learn how the story you are living is influenced by a set of themes that are dominant in your life at this time. These themes (archetypes) evolve and change as you live your life; they are a spiral and can be repeated many times in response to events that cause your life to shift. Understanding your true nature helps to provide insight on the unique talents that you can use to keep soaring higher and higher.

Step 3: Establish where you are stuck.

Think through prior times in your life when you attempted to change and didn't succeed. I recommend you start a change journal to record what happened and why you weren't able to be successful. Go deeper than just the surface reasons, like, "I didn't have enough time," "It was too hard," or "I lost interest," by using the following technique. Each time you make a statement, ask yourself why. For example:

"I didn't have enough time."

"Why didn't you have enough time?"

"Because I am working overtime at my job."

"Why are you working overtime at your job?"

"Because I need the job."

"Why do you need the job?"

"Because I am afraid of being without money."

"Why are you afraid of being without money?"

"Because we never had enough growing up and that makes me feel insecure."

Keep asking these questions until you arrive at a final answer that gives you an emotional basis for your actions. This is the real source of your resistance, and you will need to work on addressing it.

Step 4: Decide where you want to go.

Using the knowledge gained from the prior three steps can help you craft a vision of your new life. Once you have a vision, you are that much closer to starting to make real change.

Create a vision board that has images related to where you want to go with your changes. Put this somewhere that you can see it every day; it is a very important step to create a visual reference of your dreams.

Creating a vision board helps to call the Law of Attraction into play. Knowing "what" you want, mobilizes the universe to help you achieve the "how" to get there. Use this to guide your progress and inspire your destiny.

Step 5: Decide how you are going to get there.

Using your vision as a guide, write down one thing that you are going to do first. And then go find the solution to what you want to do. Sign up. Commit. Don't wait; otherwise, you will find reasons not to do it. Don't try to plan beyond the one thing. Just select an action that starts to move you in the right direction. It may not be exactly right, but it is a start. All you need right now is to start something that will—hopefully—spark your passion.

Choose a quote or mantra that represents what your vision for the change is or an inspiration to help keep you focused. Write or print it out, and put it up everywhere so you can see it—fridge, computer, office, bathroom mirror. Read it every day.

These steps take you through each of the stages of examining all dimensions of the uniquely beautiful self that is *you*. If any step gets too difficult, stop and unload with a sharing buddy. A sharing buddy is someone you can trust to ask frank questions and who you know will give you honest answers, unclouded by competitiveness, jealousy, or a hidden agenda. If you don't have someone you can trust, a personal coach is a great option, as personal coaches are trained to uplift and support you in your journey. They are also neutral and have no personal agendas to interfere with your progress. Having someone with whom you can share openly, honestly, and naturally is an amazing resource to help you on your way.

A human being is a part of the whole called by us universe, a part limited in time and space. He experiences himself, his thoughts and feeling as something separated from the rest, a kind of optical delusion of his consciousness. This delusion is a kind of prison for us, restricting us to our personal desires and to affection for a few persons nearest to us. Our task must be to free ourselves from this prison by widening our circle of compassion to embrace all living creatures and the whole of nature in its beauty.
—Albert Einstein

two

Renew Your Faith in the Universe

The term *universe* is used a lot in this book and appears as a tangible item in many great thinkers' works. But what is this dynamic we call the universe?

To me, the best way to describe the universe is from the Hindu and Buddhist religion. They use the word *dharma*, which has no equivalent meaning in English. The definition I like the best is this one:

dharma:

1. Hinduism and Buddhism
   a. the principle or law that orders the universe
   b. individual conduct in conformity with this principle
   c. the essential function or nature of a thing

(Source: freedictionary.com)

The reason I love this concept is because it groups together the fact that there are laws that are governing the universe and that we as individuals have a responsibility to live in accordance with them. It also brings up the idea that everything, from the universe to people to a blade of grass, has an essence that defines its true nature. This true nature is what guides the function. If we look around at the wildlife that surrounds us, we see that it operates according to its true nature or function. A tree doesn't try to be a bird or a mouse or a snake. The wild creatures also understand the principles and laws by which their functioning is governed. When the temperature drops, the tree knows for its leaves to change color and fall. You don't see the tree trying to hang on to its leaves in an attempt to be the greenest, showiest tree through the winter. There is an inherent understanding of its purpose and true nature.

People are the only species in nature that appear lost and out of touch with its purpose. We understand that we are born, grow, learn, marry, have children, and get old. However, somewhere in history, a whole other purpose was inserted in our makeup, which requires that we make as much money as we can regardless of the cost to ourselves or others and work ourselves into a stress-filled state. Was this the consequence of eating from the tree of knowledge? We think we know better than the universe and have lost our true purpose. What is it exactly that we have lost?

We have lost our understanding that our purpose on earth is to be guardians of the Garden of Eden we call earth. It is to live by a set of principles as ancient as time, which guide us on how to keep earth alive, healthy and fully functioning. As long as we do this, the earth will continue to provide for us. Dharma is derived from the word *dhr*, which means to uphold, sustain, or uplift. Sadly though, we have confused protector with owner. We see earth as ours to exploit, destroy, and use as our ego-driven selves see fit in order to keep increasing our knowledge and superiority as a species. But pride always comes before the fall; should we choose to continue blindly down this path, our children or grandchildren will have to live with the negative consequences of this choice.

You may be thinking now that this sounds like mumbo-jumbo. That is okay, because what I am talking about is a concept that requires complete faith and a large dose of lateral thinking. I am asking you to recognize that your presence on this earth is not random or meaningless. You are here to fulfill a purpose. You have an energy that you contribute to the larger whole. And this is as real as this book you are reading.

Another way of looking at this is best described by Deepak Chopra (chopra.com): "Dharma is an ancient Sanskrit word with numerous layers of meaning. It commonly refers to the universal force that guides our life and carries us safely through the threats and challenges along the way."

It is absolutely beautiful to know that we have the possibility of connecting with a force that will help us navigate challenges. The reason I prefer the Hindu perspective over the Christian is because the Christian religion does not recognize strongly enough the part that nature plays in all this. It elevates God up into the heavens. But this all-encompassing power is right here on earth and can be experienced all around us in a tangible way. Christianity also uses a threat to create compliance to principles. If you don't follow the commandments, you won't get into heaven. I am not a big believer in the use of threats to create change. Change happens when people have a personal sense of vision relating to the larger whole. If you feel like you own a piece of the vision, then you build a larger sense of accountability and have a tangible relationship with the effects of ignoring the principles.

Striving toward enlightenment is a key concept of why dharma requires the following of principles. Enlightenment is a positive goal and suggests that we all have the potential to get closer to the higher power through the transformation of our internal selves using the principles or laws laid down. It is our choice. We have the power. We are the painters of our own vision, and if we are willing to embark on an adventure, we will be the forgers of our own future and of this living, breathing universe that sustains us.

This is where karma fits in. Karma is the action that you take in order to live according to dharma. This includes actions of both the mind and body. Karma is therefore a central concept to any natural change program, as this is the energy that you expend on the steps you take to create change. If you direct your energy or action in positive directions, you will receive positive energy in turn. Likewise, if you direct your energy in a negative pursuit, negativity will be your reward. Karma includes taking the right action for yourself, others, and the universe.

This is a wonderful description of karma:

> Since kamma (karma) is an invisible force, we cannot see it working with our physical eyes. To understand how kamma works, we can compare it to seeds: the results of kamma are stored in the subconscious mind in the same way as the leaves, flowers, fruits and trunk of a tree are stored in its seed. Under favorable conditions, the fruits of kamma will be produced just as with moisture and light, the leaves and trunk of a tree will sprout from its tiny seed.
>
> (Source: Budsas.org)

There are a number of different laws of karma; the ones I want to highlight are as follows:

1. The Law of Cause and Effect (The Great Law)

"As you sow, so shall you reap." (Bible, Galations VI, King James Version) Whatever you want to manifest for yourself in your life, you need to practice integrating that into how you live your life. If you are struggling with an issue and you want others to be empathetic and kind, then you need to be empathetic and kind to others. If you want people's support in your change, you need to offer them support. If you need positive energy, then provide positive energy.

2. The Law of Change

This law in essence says that history will keep repeating itself until we learn the lessons we need to in order to change our path in life. Do you keep dating the wrong kind of man or woman? Do you keep losing jobs? Do you keep thinking that life is unfair? If this is your life, then you need to figure out what it is that you need to learn in order to stop the pattern.

3. The Law of Responsibility

This requires recognizing that if there is something wrong in our lives, there is no one else responsible but ourselves. We own the accountability for what is or isn't in our lives.

4. The Law of Patience and Reward

You have to earn the reward through hard work and patience, believing that it will happen.

5. The Law of Growth

In order to grow, it is not that others around us need to change. It is we who need to expand and exercise control over how we evolve.

6. The Law of Connection

Nothing stands alone. Every little thing, no matter how small, is connected to the whole. Each person we meet, book we read, training we take, or place we go has a connection to our journey in a way that is hard to understand at the time. We mustn't doubt that small steps are important to our journey.

7. The Law of Here and Now

The past is the past, and it should stay there. Being trapped in the past through rethinking old thoughts, recreating old behaviors, or reliving past events keeps us from being fully present in the here and now.

8. The Law of Attraction

Your thoughts become things. Whatever you think about your life will be the reality. You need to project positive thoughts in order to receive positive results. Be clear in what you want to achieve to open up the channel for the universe to manifest your desires.

Wild with the Universe Principles

I believe in and will practice the Laws of the Universe.

I strive to put only positive energy into
the world as much as possible.

I have faith that there is a plan and purpose
for each and every one of us.

I take ownership of understanding how I need to
grow from changes that are beyond my control.

I will stay strong in my belief in my vision of life and
take proactive changes to make it a reality.

Your Change Strategy

Step 1: Start a gratitude journal.

Gratitude is one of the most powerful habits you can develop in your life. It truly is a virtue; by practicing it regularly, you can open up the channel to the universe. It keeps you rooted in your humility and your thankfulness for all of the gifts you have been granted. Think about the following few concepts as the basis of all gratitude:

- We are alive and breathing.

The human body is a small miracle of incredible complexity and resilience. Honor the gift it gives you by keeping the store that is your life open and thriving.

- We get to live on earth.

I never cease to be amazed that we get to live on the only known life-sustaining planet in the universe. Imagine if we got to be a bacterium lurking on an inhospitable planet. That would suck.

- Our planet is a Garden of Eden.

Beauty is all around us. It nurtures us. Feeds us. Gives us air to breathe and water to drink. And we live in a time of balanced temperatures which is way better than living in the days of the ice age.

- We have other living, breathing creations to love and play with.

Some drive us crazy. Some we lose, which is painful. But we get to experience emotions and feelings, which are a gift in themselves.

- We are free to live life however we choose.

Each and every person has so many dimensions that make up his or her uniqueness. Freedom of choice gives us a path of continued growth should we choose to keep expanding and exploring all of who we can be.

Write in your journal every day what you are grateful for. Eventually, you will find that the happiness overflows out of you as you focus on the positives and celebrate all the simple things.

As you find happiness in every moment, take that and pass it on to someone who may need that lightness and brightness.

Step 2: Find a gratitude stone.

A gratitude stone is a very important part of my gratitude practice. It is a very real element of the earth, which reminds me of the power of nature. You don't have to find the stone; you will be drawn to it. When you are out communing with nature, shift your vision so that you are seeing every detail of the landscape. Notice that swirl of sand, the interestingly shaped tree, the insect walking across the path, or the water coursing over the rocks. Recognize the beauty in it so that your mind can open up to feeling your connection to the earth. As you gaze around, a stone will catch your eye and stand out from all the others. That is your gratitude stone. I carry mine around in my purse so that I see it each day I open it.

My husband actually found his stone before I found mine, and without me even realizing it, he took it with him every day and recited daily what he was grateful for. He found it in a river in October, and in December, we sat down and wrote our goals together to engage the Law of Attraction. He is an architect and was very unhappy working for somebody else, as the company was cutting his hours and he felt like he wasn't being true to his talents. He clearly documented that he wanted his own firm and all the details of what that firm looked like. In January, we agreed he would embark on a very definite conscious change step and leave his job to start his own firm. We understood the challenges that would go along with that but knew we had to take the first step. In February, I was searching a national website for businesses for sale that I might set up once he was established. And right there in front of me was a listing for an architecture firm for sale in our city. My husband was reluctant at first to purchase a firm, as that is not the normal course of how professional firms are transitioned. But he agreed to go and meet with the owner. Six months later, he was the proud owner of a firm that fit, exactly to the letter, every criteria he had laid out.

The power of a tiny stone and a humble heart cannot be underestimated.

Step 3: Write down what you want.

The story above illustrates the power of the Law of Attraction. It is working constantly to bring your thoughts into reality, and you get to decide what those thoughts are.

Find an afternoon that you can dedicate to *yourself.* Put on some meditative music (download or you can find a radio station online that will play songs continuously). Light some aromatic candles or incense, and wear comfortable clothes.

Pull out your vision that you wrote in Stage 1. Read it a few times, and let the words sink in.

Then write down on a piece of paper what your "why" is. Your "why" is the reason that you care deeply about creating the change you want to make. It is what is going to be the fuel to drive you closer to where you want to be. It will provide you with the courage to push through your fears and take the leaps that are necessary to keep escalating your life toward your vision.

Once you have your "why" written down, take another piece of paper and write down "what" you want. Your "what" doesn't have to be huge initially. In fact, the simpler it is, the better. You have to be able to define it in terms that are very clear and precise. This is your blueprint for the universe. It can be large or small so long as you can make it very real.

- Is it to be happier?
- Is it to be a better person for your children?
- Is it to get healthier?
- Is it to help others less fortunate?

Put your vision, why, and what together in front of you and read them together. If you are smiling at the end of reading them, then you have captured the essence of your shift well. If you are unsure, then do this exercise again, trying other "why's" and "what's". Oftentimes, the biggest barrier to taking a step toward change is that you create goals that are based on what you believe others expect you should want. Figuring out what you want and why, is the hardest step. This is why you have to not just *think* it but *feel* it. If you are not feeling it, you will not live it and will give up when change starts getting challenging, which is absolutely going to happen.

Repeat this over until you have the level of commitment described earlier in the book—the strength of conviction that this is absolutely the right path for you and that you will not waver if anyone questions why you are doing it, tries to pull you down, or makes you feel like you won't succeed.

Write your vision, what, and why on a large piece of paper on your wall and small notes to post where you can see them every day. You are going to need to live and breathe the new reality you are laying out for yourself. Use your change journal to record your thoughts and feelings about what you have defined. The gratitude journal should only be filled with positive thoughts; however, your change journal is a place to put any thoughts that cross your mind, whether negative or positive. A good practice is to write whatever enters your head first thing in the morning, as it is a very fertile time for creative thoughts to bubble from your subconscious mind to your conscious mind. Often, ideas or motivations come to you in the form of dreams, and if you capture them, they can provide additional strength of purpose as you start to imagine your shifted self.

Step 4: Join a yoga practice.

Yoga is a magical thing. It is a spiritual, physical, and mental endeavor all beautifully blended into one. Feeling stressed? Yoga will leave you floating in a sea of tranquility. Feeling sore? Yoga will iron out the kinks and get your body feeling flexible again. Looking to reconnect with your wild soul? Yoga will remove you from the real world and transport you to a realm where you are in a safe, dark womb of stillness and can start tuning in to your intuitive self.

Even if you just start at home or follow a yoga class online, it still has amazing benefits. I tend to look for classes that have a strong spiritual component, as I use yoga as my source of meditation.

Step 5: Learn to meditate.

A large part of this journey to change is about inner reflection and growth. Meditation is a tool to aid you with quieting your mind to allow you to go into a place that is not overrun with stress, distractions, to-do lists, and past conversations. Try this meditation in nature. You can do it while drinking your tea in the morning or on a park bench at lunch or in the evening as you savor the drawing to a close of the day.

This is a wonderful meditation I use from Meditation Oasis (meditationoasis.com):

Basic Nature Meditation—Eyes Closed

> Find a comfortable position sitting or lying down. Begin with a few deep breaths, breathing deep into the belly, to help you relax and to bring you to the sensations of the present moment. Now close your eyes and be present to what is being experienced with your eyes closed. Notice how your body feels, as well as the activity of your mind and emotions. Experience whatever is present without resisting anything or trying to change it. Do this for about a minute.

> Now bring your awareness to everything that you can experience in your surroundings. Feel the temperature of the air on your skin, the feeling of the breeze and the sun. Notice the sounds around you—birds, bees, crickets, flowing water. Listen to the symphony of nature. For the rest of the meditation, continue to experience these feelings and sounds. Whenever your mind wanders, gently bring it back to the experience of nature.

> As you meditate, you can see where your attention is naturally drawn or purposefully scan for different experiences. You can also focus on one experience and notice the experience in greater detail. If it is a bird's song, notice the quality of the sound, as if you are going more deeply into the sound. (It may seem to have a shape or texture.) Don't analyze the sound and label it with your mind; simply notice the quality of it.

Once again, whenever you notice that the mind has become absorbed in thoughts, easily bring it back to the sounds and sensations of being in nature. At times, both awareness of the sensations from the environment and thoughts will be present. That's fine. Just savor the experiences of nature.

The clearest way into the Universe is
through a forest wilderness.
—John Muir

three

Reconnect with Nature

We are energetic beings who thrive off positive energy. Yet we have forgotten how to plug in to the largest power source there is: *nature*.

The first time I felt the intensity of the earth's energy was a truly electric experience for me (pun intended). I was on a trip to a lodge in Zambia to write an article for the magazine I worked for. As we crossed the mighty Zambezi River on a small and rickety ferry, I became aware of a pounding vibration in my chest. It wasn't my heartbeat, but the only way to describe it is as a steady throb that pounded in tandem with my heart.

Over the course of the days I spent at the lodge, the sensation intensified, and I found my level of excitement grew at the same rate. Every cell in my body was thrumming as though it had only just realized it was alive. Every experience, animal, and person I engaged with glowed with an intensity that I now recognize was their energy field, which I was feeling. I felt drunk with the energy overload, and it kept intensifying as nature put on an amazing show for me. I rafted class-5 rapids below Victoria Falls, canoed upriver, hugged baobab trees, and wrestled with tiger fish. I felt high from the sunsets, the likes of which I had ever only seen in paintings, and walked to the edge of the greatest falls in Africa, *Mosi oa Tunya*, the Smoke that Thunders, where I thought my chest would burst with the force of energy coursing through my entire body. It was nature on steroids.

The reason this experience was so powerful is because the energy in Africa is still very raw. It is where we originated from and has a special energy, which has, for many generations, been relatively untainted by modern encroachments. I love leading trips to Africa to give people a taste of the raw beauty. I have not met one person who hasn't been moved by the vibe and energy of humankind's first home.

If I hadn't already realized that this trip was a turning point for me, the fact that one night I looked up and witnessed a huge orange total lunar eclipse was a sign that something magical had happened and the universe was encouraging me to start my change journey toward my one true purpose in life. It made me question everything about my life to date.

I almost changed everything in my life after that trip. I felt so connected to nature, the animals, and the people around me that it stirred a restlessness in me that eventually took me half-way around the world. I understood what my wild self was telling me. I wanted to study to be an environmentalist and go live in the African bush communing with nature as my day-to-day job—except I already had a great life laid out for me. I was married to a wonderful man. I had a fantastic job as a managing editor of a magazine and a beautiful home. Everything was perfect—except my soul.

Everyone I told my ideas to, seemed to think I was crazy. When I mentioned nature was my church, I got strange looks. So I decided that this was just a whim and that everyone else was right. I chose to ignore the message from the universe. I shut down the intuition of my soul and stuck to the path laid out for me. I turned my back on my wild nature and in the process lost myself for many years.

Fortunately, the universe never gives up sending us signals that remind us of our calling in life. These are evident in the coincidences constantly happening; they are really messages to us to take in and figure out how to understand. We can find them in the feeling of knowing we experience when we meet someone who is going to play a pivotal role in our life or in the opportunities that appear that can take our life in a completely different direction if we choose to let them.

Eventually, we can't help but notice that there is a pattern emerging as our true nature keeps making its presence felt. Being in nature increases our abilities to tune in to that intuition, as we have a free flow of energy between us and the wildness.

Wild Nature Principles

Nature is my energy source.

In nature, I can be closest to the highest power
in the universe, whatever I call it.

I have a relationship with all natural beings.

It is my responsibility to sustain nature.

I will practice a life of minimalism rather than
materialism to preserve natural resources.

Your Change Strategy

Try each of these experiences and record how you feel in your change journal:

Step 1: Experience water.

The easiest way to start consciously feeling the earth's energy and your reaction to it is to sit next to a waterfall. Find a waterfall near your home, no matter how big or small, and sit comfortably in a safe place near to it. Close your eyes, and focus on the sensory cues you are receiving. As you hear the pounding of the water hitting the rocks and feel the mist on your cheeks, you should start to experience the vibration of energy in your chest. Once this happens, you have connected with the water's energy and you will recognize that the water is alive and vibrant.

Start breathing deeply, expanding your chest as you do so. If you are fortunate enough to live near a waterfall that is safe to swim by, you will be able to intensify this experience a thousand fold. Always practice safe swimming, and don't get too close. Swim near the falls, and depending on how high it is, you will feel the waves of energy pounding on your chest. The best experience I had of this was in Havasu Canyon in Arizona. The Mooney Falls is 190 feet high, and we could not even get close to the falls the intensity was so great. I threw my arms back and just worshipped this wonder of nature, allowing the energy to consume me. That was a magical experience.

Waterfalls and ocean waves give off negative ions that charge the atmosphere and generate a physical energy force. Ions are molecules that have gained or lost an electrical charge. They are created in nature as air molecules break apart because of sunlight, radiation, and moving air and water. The air in natural settings is said to contain tens of thousands of negative ions, as opposed to your home or office, which may have none or a few hundred at most.

"The action of the pounding surf creates negative air ions and we also see it immediately after spring thunderstorms when people report lightened moods," says ion researcher Michael Terman, PhD, of Columbia University in New York.

The Columbia University studies of people affected by seasonal affective disorder and depression show that negative ion generators offer a benefit equal to that of pharmaceutical antidepressants. "The best part is that there are relatively no side effects, but we still need to figure out appropriate doses and which people it works best on," he says.

"Generally speaking, negative ions increase the flow of oxygen to the brain; resulting in higher alertness, decreased drowsiness, and more mental energy," says Pierce J. Howard, PhD, author of *The Owner's Manual for the Brain: Everyday Applications from Mind Brain Research.*

Step 2: Experience the wind.

Ah, my second favorite natural experience! Wind has the ability to caress and arouse restlessness. The best way to reacquaint yourself with our friend the wind is to go sailing. Try to find a largish sailboat (thirty-four feet and above) where you have the opportunity to stand in the bow, Titanic style. Fling your arms wide, and let the wind rush over you, lift your hair like you were flying, and make you feel one with its power. If you can't find a sailboat owner to let you sail with him or her, you can even commune with a gentle breeze experienced on a beautiful day. To know you have really felt it, you should feel a tingling on your skin, maybe your hair will rise a bit, and a sense of anticipation will rush to your belly. Wind is about action and yearning for more experiences.

Step 3: Be with the trees.

It is proven that trees give off an organic compound called phytoncides (wood essential oils) that have a positive effect on hormones and blood pressure, as well as immune and cellular responses. Exposure to natural spaces also offers protective factors against depression and anxiety. And, of course, the oxygen boost you get from being surrounded by oxygen-producing pow-erhouses is like candy for your cells.

Researchers have studied the effects of shinrin-yoku or for-est bathing, a popular pursuit in Japan, on immune function in a study called "Effect of Forest Bathing Trips on Immune Function". The study looked into whether forest bathing increases the activity of people's natural killer (NK) cells, a component of the immune system that fights cancer. In two studies, small groups of men and women respectively were assessed before and after a two-night/three-day forest-bath-ing trip. During the trips, the subjects went on three forest walks and stayed in a hotel in the forest. Blood tests were taken before and after the trip, revealing a significant boost in NK activity in the subjects in both groups. The increase was observed as long as thirty days after the trip. Follow-up studies showed a significant increase in NK activity was also achieved after a day trip to a forest, with the increase observed for seven days after the trip.

The idea behind forest bathing is to let nature enter your body through all of your five senses.

Find a walk or hike through the forest, and breathe deep, yogic breaths to inhale the rich air of the trees. A sense of calm should come over you as you unplug from the electronic world and plug into the natural world. Aim to go into natural spaces at least two to three times a week.

Step 4: Spend time in the sun.

The sun is our life-giving force. The life of every creature on the planet depends on the sun's energy. Prana is described as life force energy, and we gain this from the sun.

The sun is the fire of nature and has a hypnotic quality that mesmerizes us with its energy. The sun has been used for genera-tions as a source of healing, as in the yogic science of sunbathing, which is called *atapa snana*. While we need to limit our exposure to the sun, we do need to absorb sunlight, as our body requires it for the very critical production of vitamin D. Everything in moderation is a good rule to follow.

Make sure to enjoy and celebrate the beneficial qualities of the sun for short periods a few times a week.

Step 5: Explore the benefits of rock—quartz.

Quartz is considered a master stone that helps to amplify your energies. Having a strong sense of energy will help you feel connected to the earth and give you strength to move forward with change.

I have a smaller quartz crystal stone that I keep near me, and I am fortunate enough to live in an area where it is plentiful in my garden. I have it positioned in areas throughout the yard to keep our home bathed in a pool of positive natural energy. I even keep a piece in my car.

We need the tonic of wildness…At the same time that we are earnest to explore and learn all things, we require that all things be mysterious and unexplorable, that land and sea be indefinitely wild, unsurveyed and unfathomed by us because unfathomable. We can never have enough of nature.
—Henry David Thoreau, *Walden: Or, Life in the Woods*

Stage 2 of Change

The Seedling

Once you have decided that change has to happen, you move into the cycle of contemplating the right way to create change. This is a stage of trial and error as you test out different options to take you where you need to go. Typically, in this stage, you have to make a concrete step toward something, regardless of whether it is the right path to avoid cycling back to stage 1.

Life is a series of spirals. You start on a path and follow it. If it is a positive path, it will continue to grow and expand so that you never reach the end of that spiral. If it is a negative path, you will reach the end of the spiral, at which time, growth will stop and the spiral will go into a downward cycle. You are then faced with two choices: change, or stay where you are. If you choose to change, you have two options for how you achieve it. In the spirit of growth and learning, you can opt to retrace your path to establish where you made choices that led to the contraction of your life spiral. This path is recommended if your intuition tells you this is the right path but you are manifesting elements of it that are not true to your wild nature. It carries less stress and is a good choice if you are not in a secure place and need to preserve elements of your current life to maintain your basic needs, because making large changes would put you or your loved ones at an unacceptable risk.

The second choice for change is to abandon this spiral completely and make a radical leap into a new life path. This can be a heady alternative if you are feeling strong and you know with every fiber of your being that your prior path was damaging to you. Some paths can keep destroying you if you don't stop the downward spiral. This approach requires you to have a plan to ensure you have a means of maintaining your basic needs while you transition. This is very much the adventurous change, as you will have to deal with a great deal of risk, personal challenge, and uncertainty. Your reserves of faith need to be deep and strong to sustain you when you inevitably start to doubt if you made the right choice. Doubt is a normal part of change, as it is your mind challenging your intuition on its choices. Don't view doubt as a negative. Instead, see it as a way to sharpen your intuition and reaffirm through examination of your choices that you do indeed trust your intuition's guidance.

Conscious change is never easy but is preferable to the alternative, which is crisis change. Should you choose to ignore the call to change and instead stay in that negative place, you will be faced with a crisis. Crisis is the mechanism by which the universe propels you toward a quantum leap out of the negative cycle into a new spiral of growth. The experience is generally not pleasant, but it is the jolt to allow you to reset the principles by which you live your life. Choose to recreate the same spiral you had before, and you will end up at the same end point. When crisis forces you into change, it is important to learn from the past experience by setting new principles more aligned with natural living. As you do this, your spiral will expand.

This is a basic principle of universal energy. For balance to be maintained, all things should be in a positive state of energy production. A natural correction takes place when negativity starts to upset the balance. This principle is true of humans and the larger earth. The more negative our impact on the earth, the more likely a quantum leap of massive proportions will be.

Oftentimes, the first step you need to take (whether due to conscious or crisis change) is to improve your diet. Change becomes much harder when you are fighting with low energy and fatigue from poor eating choices. The pursuit of change is about the achievement of harmony with the universal energy. This harmony needs to be internal and external. You need to look at what is initially within your control to change to create a fertile earth within you in which your change seedling can grow.

Whether you decide to cut out fast food or take a healthy-eating course, there has to be a tangible step to demonstrate you have the commitment. Even if you don't believe it wholeheartedly or have resistance or fear still present, you can't look backward to the rut. You are starting to move in the right direction and can't be tempted to give up. During this stage, you are not likely to land in the perfect place, as this is very much a transition period. Everything will feel difficult, as you are likely struggling with the baggage of the past, which is weighing you down. But you have to take the first step toward change.

I may never have rediscovered my wild nature if it weren't for a chance meeting at a work conference that I believe was a signal from the universe. I met someone who also believed that nature was our church and completely understood all of the beliefs I had kept shut inside of me because people around me didn't understand my connection with all things natural. That was the catalyst for me to decide that regardless of who I let down, I had to rediscover my true path.

I started by getting back to who I thought I was, back to that child who had spent every waking hour barefoot in nature. Those were my idyllic years, and while I didn't at the time know why those were the best years of my life, I just knew I needed to return to that state of bliss. I deliberately didn't buy a TV and spent the evening hours reading books to make sense of life, learning how to be independent, and getting outside. I joined an outdoor group and fell back in love with myself as the hiker, sailor, kayaker, and camper of my youth.

This was my second cycle of change.

⊷⊶

A seed does not have an easy time of it. It has no choice where it lands. It may get eaten by a bird, land in rocky soil, or have no water. But be inspired by the perseverance of the seedlings. They grow in cracks of rocks and sidewalks, not letting their difficult start in life stop them from the ever-important first stages of growth. Be gentle with yourself, as this is a huge upheaval and requires grit to get through. Find support to help you stay true to your commitment. Baby steps are all that is required, so long as you keep toddling forward.

The fairest thing in nature, a flower, still
has its roots in earth and manure.
—D.H. Lawrence

four

Release Your Inner Adventurer

Ruts are very, very comfortable. The problem with comfortable is that you are stationary. Your body needs movement, both literally and figuratively. Growth does not happen on the sofa while you watch other people's adventures unfold on TV or social media.

Courage is one of the cornerstones of change. Assess what your groove looks like and decide if that is truly what your soul needs. Be brave enough to admit you need more, and then take a step to test your ability to break out of the box you find yourself in. Commit to an adventure outside of your comfort zone. Maybe you walk the greenway, book a whitewater rafting trip, or set a goal to climb Kilimanjaro in five years. These physical actions will move your mind and your body forward on a growth path that will surprise you with just what you are truly capable of.

Adventure is a catalyst and a training ground for change. When you embark on an adventure, you employ all three of your resources of mind, body, and soul. Take, for example, a backpacking trip. Your mind is engaged in planning and rationalizing the route you are going to take, deciding what supplies you need, and figuring out the logistics of getting there. Your body needs to be in great shape to carry your pack each day and get you to where you need to be. Your soul is engaged in the desire to go to the wilderness. After all, it is a mental and physical challenge that you could easily bail on, as you may convince yourself it falls into the too-hard category. However, with your soul being engaged, you imagine what it will feel like to camp in the woods with no one around, how the earth will smell after it rains, the brightness of the stars without light pollution, and the joy of no computers or cell phones draining your energy. And with those soul musings, you are drawn to want to experience it, and that is what provides the desire to take the adventure.

With adventure, you have to muster a lot of your mental resources that don't get called on often if you live in a comfortable, convenient, and supposedly civilized country—your courage, your grit, your survival skills, your mastery of fear, and your ability to let go of the innate need for control that everyone has, in favor of an out-of-control environment where, at any time, circumstances can change and it will be down to you and you alone to triumph. You are responsible for every decision you make.

On one backpacking trip, the heavens opened halfway up the mountain. That in itself was a pleasure, as hiking in the rain instantly transports you to the child that you were, who loved jumping in puddles and playing in the rain. Where the adventure got interesting and called all of those aforementioned skills into play was when we got to a river crossing. Half of our party had crossed the river five minutes prior. In that short time, a flash flood coursed down the mountain, swelling the river to a raging torrent. We had a decision to make: turn around and miss out on a trip that only happens once a year if you win a highly sought-after place in a lodge on the top of the mountain or find a way through the river.

We chose to face the challenge head-on and opted for the choice that was risky but offered the greatest potential. We chose to cross the river. This was no simple decision, as the river dropped off the side of the mountain to form a waterfall about ten feet from where we were proposing to cross. We found a branch (which in hindsight was rather flimsy), set it across the river, and waded across with the current trying to pull our feet out from under us with every step. At one point, it almost succeeded as I was wading across. I felt my feet slide out from under me and knew that after a certain point, I would be gone. The fear I felt was like none other as I faced the fact that I would die.

Fortunately for me, part of our risk-mitigation strategy was to have strong male friends on each side of the river, and a friend stepped in to stop my slide. I lived to tell the tale but learned many lessons from that experience about how we could better prepare for the challenges of adventure—and life.

Take adventures to get yourself into the wild and reunite with your childlike spirit, who rejoices in being dirty and outside. Nature is a great teacher and is the master of change to promote new growth. Take lessons from your adventures that you can use to aid you as you face change. Be bold, but be prepared. Be courageous, but be careful. Be adventurous, but be adaptable. Above all, have a great support network and never stop learning from experience.

Wild Life Principles

Everything is an adventure.

Every month, I will try something new or different.

Getting dirty and sweaty is a good thing;
looking perfect is a bad thing.

Adrenaline from adventure reminds you that you are alive.

Dancing, skipping or singing is required at least once a month.

Your Change Strategy

Step 1: View the world like a child does.

Think back to when you were a child. Do you remember how excited you got with new experiences? How thrilled you were to be getting dirty and playing outside? The next time it rains, I want you to go outside barefoot and get wet. Put your feet in the wet earth, and wiggle them around. Feel the wet sod sticking between your toes. Spin around, laugh, and rejoice as your hair gets wet. This is living.

Step 2: Go barefoot whenever you can.

Our ancestors all walked around barefoot, as it offered a direct connection between their bodies and the earth's energy. We are electrical beings who need to recharge through direct connection with the earth's electromagnetic energy. This is called earthing. According to Dr. Stephen Sinatra, by practicing earthing, we soak electrons up into the body, which thins the blood and also discharges the free radicals that have built up. He also suggests that this shifts the autonomic nervous system and provides optimal homeostasis, which is the ability of the body to provide internal stability in the face of disturbance.

I never wear shoes in the house and regularly walk barefoot outdoors. I don't use chemicals on my lawn, so I can do this at home. If your lawn is going to need a toxic cleanse from all the chemicals you have been using on it, I would suggest leaving it a year before you walk barefoot on it. My best suggestion for enjoying being barefoot is to spend time at the beach or in a grassy meadow where you know it is relatively untouched by humans. That great feeling of recharging you get from your beach vacation likely has earthing as the simple source of bliss.

Step 3: Learn to love your wild and natural look.

One of the greatest compliments I ever received was that I had the best hiking hair. Hiking hair is what your hair looks like after it has been rained on, tied up, shoved into a hat, and then let loose without brushing to bounce around in a natural fuzz. I never wear makeup and instead get a little sun-kissed to bring natural color to my face.

The secret to learning to love your wild and natural look? Don't look in the mirror. I mean, you can look to make sure you have nothing stuck between your teeth or to give a cursory glance at what is happening on your face. But don't look in the mirror to overanalyze what is happening. As soon as you start criticizing what you see, you will get caught up in the need to be perfectly turned out. I adopt the same approach that most men take as they are fortunate to have less social pressure than women. You don't see them examining each wrinkle, cursing over every spot, or ironing their hair to make it stay in one place. They accept themselves as they are (unless they are a narcissist of course) which is what every wild being, men and women, should aspire to be able to do.

We were all born with a slew of talents, and our fixation on beauty as the most important one is ridiculously sad. We should care more about our inner beauty than our outer beauty.

I challenge you to cover all your mirrors for a month and be courageous in putting yourself out there without makeup. Limit yourself to five minutes of grooming time. It may seem trivial, but it is an important step in acknowledging and bringing to life our wild one. When we try to change how we look, we are in essence rejecting our true selves. We are saying that we are not good enough, and that spills over into all areas of our life. You are good enough. In fact, you are more than good enough. You just have to let go of artifice and grab hold of adventure by being completely and utterly naturally you. Anyone who values you by your looks is operating from a shallow perspective and is exerting control over your true nature. Be stronger than that, and fall in love with yourself in all your natural glory. Once you are able to do that, you should be able to find a happy mid-point where you use some enhancement to fulfill the expectations of your job, or your own idea of what looks best for you to feel confident, without being a slave to Botox or the latest cosmetic.

Step 4: Plan an adventure.

Start with a simple adventure but one that requires you to move outside of your comfort zone. Whitewater rafting is a great first option, as it is friendly for most age groups and skill levels and does not require you to purchase any specialized equipment. It gives you the benefit of being up close and personal with nature, and it requires you to use body and mind to anticipate how to ride the waves and engage a level of courage to overcome the fear of falling out of the boat. The best reason why this is a great first adventure is that after you have tamed the river (and your own fear of it) you get a natural high, which makes you feel energized to take on more adventure activities. Visit naturalwonderstours.com for more ideas.

Step 5: Live outside the box.

Being silly is an important step in letting go of our preconceived selves. When you are doing something that others may judge or that may make them wonder about your sanity, you are doing wonderful soul work. Letting go of what others think of you is part of the adventure in forging your own path. When you try to live a life that is designed to please others or act according to a set of unspoken societal rules, then you are shutting down your natural instincts in favor of following pack rules.

Be different. Be quirky. Be nonconformist. Nobody lays down the rules. Fitting in may be easier by following the rules, but if you are fitting in with others' external pressure, you are likely falling out with your own internal pleasure. The following are some ways you can start to be yourself:

- Experiment with how you like to dress.
- Test out what style of living works for you.
- Determine what food you like to eat.
- Find places you like to hang out.
- Make friends with people who make you laugh.
- Dance around like a mad thing to an unknown song that nobody else may like but totally makes you feel wild.
- Sing in the car, in the shower, in the grocery store—wherever you desire.

Learn to love people giving you weird looks for not fitting in. This is the highest compliment you can receive; it means you are getting closer to knowing your wild one.

Praised be my Lord, for our sister water.
—St Francis of Assisi

five

Reset Your Body

Like no other time in history, our bodies are assaulted each and every minute of the day with toxins. They are all around us and yet are hidden out of sight.

We breathe them in from the harsh chemicals we use in our home and those that companies release into the air and water. We absorb them through our skin from using products to repel mosquitoes, chemical cocktails of beauty products, and unplanned exposure to lawn and bug poisons. Who hasn't sprayed to kill weeds and accidentally gotten some on your hand or foot? And worst of all, we eat them from the pesticides sprayed on our produce, to the coatings in our cookware, and the leaching into our water from plastic.

Face the facts. Your body is toxic. And if you are toxic, you can imagine what happens to our children, who start out with this overload from birth and then get further exposed.

This step in the program is an important one to lay the foundation for what you are going to be building as you work your way through the book. Everything I suggest is very simple, as I don't believe in overwhelming people with complex rituals or routines that are not easy to integrate into their daily lives. I know for a fact that all of these work.

When I was struggling with Lyme disease, one of the largest issues was that as the bacteria are killed, the body gets overwhelmed with a huge die-off that overwhelms the lymph system. It can't work fast enough to remove the toxins, and the danger, if you don't remove them, is that they will build up and delay healing. I followed these five practices every day and honestly believe they were the difference between recovering from Lyme disease and having it hang around for years, as some people experience.

Your lymphatic system is a complex drainage system that flows around your body and is responsible for eliminating cellular waste products from your tissues. To keep this system functioning optimally it is important to detox to clear waste and toxins. A clogged lymphatic system can lead to inflammation and disease.

Before you start with your detox, it is important to center your mind. This path you are starting on is a promise you are making to yourself. It is your commitment to honoring your body as a beautiful creation that should be nurtured, nourished, and sustained to allow it to function optimally. Your body is ultimately the source of your energy and chi. A wild body is a clean body. You wouldn't walk around with dirt on your face and mud on your legs, would you? (Well, unless you were adventuring, of course.) So too should you think about the inside of your body. You are carrying toxins around inside, and these are smudgy marks on your inner reflection. Consider this a body cleanse to clean up your inner workings to be in line with your outer self.

Wild Body Principles

My body is perfect on the exterior, no matter what it may look like or what you may think about it.

My body doesn't need changing but needs supporting to function optimally.

My body must be free from chemical overload.

My body must be free from heavy-metal poisoning.

My body must have a healthy lymphatic system.

Your Change Strategy

Step 1: Take Epsom salt baths.

This is the easiest detox routine to introduce. Buy a big bag of Epsom salts at the pharmacy, and take hot baths as often as you need with a cup of salts. I would aim for a bath once a week, as it is a great detoxifier, helping to draw toxins out of your body. You also absorb magnesium from Epsom salts, which is a benefit, as many people are deficient without realizing it.

Step 2: Drink warm lemon water.

Lemons, in my opinion, are one of nature's secret weapons in your healthy-living arsenal. If you do nothing else for your health, do start your day with half a lemon squeezed in warm water. Our bodies are constantly exposed to toxins, and our poor liver works overtime trying to clear these. Lemon water also aids digestion and gives you a boost of vitamin C, and there is some evidence to suggest it balances the body's pH. At first thought, you may think that a lemon would have an acidic pH, and you would be right. But the pH nature changes during the body's metabolic process, and it becomes alkaline, which is believed to be the ideal state for the body to ward off disease. I drink this every morning, and my body just loves it.

Step 3: Alternate between hot and cold showers.

For a morning boost and detox, try alternating hot and cold water. Start by making the water hot, and then switch it over to cold and back to hot as often as you can bear for up to seven times. This stimulates the lymphatic system, which allows toxins to leave the body. End with cold water. A little brrr in winter but you will feel a lovely glow after.

Step 4: Get massages.

Massage is a crucial part of my monthly routine. It has many wonderful benefits, including lymph drainage, pain relief, immunity boost, and a wonderful feeling of relaxation and stress relief.

Find a good massage therapist with whom you feel comfortable and who has the right amount of pressure to meet your comfort level.

Step 5: Use a Far Infrared Sauna.

If you are serious about detoxing and are willing to make an investment, I highly recommend a Far Infrared Sauna. I use this on a daily basis. It was a huge benefit in detoxing from Lyme disease. I saw a definite improvement in how I felt after a twenty-minute session in my sauna.

Far infrared rays are the main energy source that comes from the sun. These are the rays we don't see that warm our skin when we sit in direct sunshine. Unlike a traditional sauna, which heats the room, far infrared waves heat the tissues below the skin.

I use a portable sauna that is small enough to set up in my bedroom.

Here are some reasons I love it:

- Detoxification—the infrared heat stimulates your lymphatic system and gets you sweating. Perspiration is the body's way of clearing toxins. You will love how good you feel after.
- Cell health—the waves also stimulate the circulatory system and allow for more oxygen to flow to cells to allow them to function optimally.
- Relaxation—I start each morning with a session in the sauna. I do meditation and deep breathing exercises to help relax my mind.
- Weight loss—while that was not my goal, I definitely noticed a loss of weight. A study published in the *Journal of the American Medical Association* (1981) showed that an infrared sauna session can burn upwards of six hundred calories. Sweating causes an increase in heart rate, metabolic rate and therefore consumes energy.
- Improved circulation—this is especially good for those immobilized by illness (check with your doctor first to see if it is suitable for you); a session in the far sauna

produces an increase in blood flow equivalent to an exercise session.

- Pain relief—the heat penetrates muscles and joints to help relieve aches. Studies done with rheumatoid arthritis sufferers have shown a reduction in pain symptoms.
- Reduced seasonal affective disorder (SAD)

My top tips for safety:

- Check with your doctor before starting any kind of sauna treatment especially if you are on a medication, are under a doctor's care or have a chronic disease or condition like a heart condition, multiple sclerosis, hemophilia, hyperthyroidism, systemic lupus erythematous or adrenal suppression. People who regularly use alcohol or drugs should not use saunas.
- People at risk should not use a sauna. These include children; the elderly; women who are pregnant, nursing or menstruating; if you have implants, a pacemaker, artificial joints or metal pins.
- Research your options to find one with the lowest levels of EMF (electromagnetic field).
- Make sure to drink two to four glasses of water after to balance the loss of fluid.
- Shower directly after the sauna to ensure toxins don't get reabsorbed.
- Keep your sessions short. Daily sessions of fifteen to twenty minutes are sufficient to get the benefits. Stay alert during your session and ensure to get a sauna with a timer to keep track of how long you have been in there.
- If you feel faint or dizzy or are not sweating despite the heat, get out of the sauna and consult your doctor.

If you truly get in touch with a piece of carrot, you get in touch with the soil, the rain, the sunshine. You get in touch with Mother Earth and eating in such a way, you feel in touch with true life, your roots, and that is meditation. If we chew every morsel of our food in that way we become grateful and when you are grateful, you are happy.
—Thich Nhat Hanh

six

Refresh Your Diet

In my evaluation, 90 percent of what supermarkets stock on their shelves as food is not food. It is processed, engineered, profit-making, addiction-forming junk that is a direct path to disease. For your body to thrive, you need to dejunk your diet. This can be a slow change of gradually introducing healthy options and phasing out unhealthy options. Once you remove the addictive food, your body will crave what nature provides in its purest form—whole food.

Changing your diet is very rooted in changing your mind. When you start to think of your body as an energetic being that needs living food in order to flourish and function optimally, it shifts how you perceive what you put in your mouth.

My journey with food started as a result of my health failing. I had to keep eliminating foods, as my body couldn't tolerate them for a reason unknown to me at the time. In my twenties, I ditched sugar and milk. In my thirties, I dropped gluten because of gluten intolerance and suspected celiac disease. After my health completely failed, I became fascinated with the link between food and health—and then horrified the more I learned about how our food is tampered with, modified, and tortured to get to our plates.

There are many facts and figures and amazing movies you can watch to educate yourself about the nightmare of food production. This is a very black-and-white change that you need to make. What we call food isn't food, so forget about shopping in about 80 percent of your regular grocery store (all the middle aisles, typically). About 10 percent of goods in the store can be used in moderation, and 10 percent is fine to consume. The simplest strategy is to avoid anything for which you don't know the journey it has taken to get to your plate. If it comes in a box or package, be cautious and read the ingredients list.

Food is fuel for your body. Be conscious of what you eat but don't beat yourself up about calories or view a little bit of cheating here and there as you failing. Being fanatical is not the goal. Focus on eating naturally, and I promise it won't be hard to achieve. After a time, you will stop craving the unhealthy food, and your body will start craving water, greens, and smoothies. I can feel my body light up with energy after I eat a salad. It sounds crazy, but it is absolutely true.

Wild Food Principles

Food should not be changed from how nature created it.

Food should be unprocessed and not made in a factory.

Food should be free from genetic modification (GMO), gluten modification, antibiotics, and growth hormones.

Food should be mostly home-cooked
and support local farmers.

Food should not be withheld to diet or starve oneself;
I will have a positive relationship with food.

Your Change Strategy

Step 1: Have a smoothie a day.

Introducing smoothies into your diet is an easy way to get your daily dose of fruit and vegetables.

Purchase a blender (even an inexpensive one will do), and make a smoothie for breakfast. You can prepare the ingredients the night before or even prepare bags of ingredients for the week and freeze them.

Don't sweat exact recipes. Experiment to find what you enjoy, as, for the most part, smoothies are very forgiving and generally always taste great.

A typical rule is:
- a half to a full cup of greens, like spinach or kale
- a half to a full cup of water or almond/coconut milk
- an antioxidant fruit (or two, there are no rules)—blueberries, strawberries, peach, mango, apple
- an energy fruit, like banana
- to make it more vegetable-based, add carrot or cucumber instead of some of the fruits

Additional supplements I recommend:
- Chia seeds—they boost energy and swell to make you feel full.
- Baobab powder—it's a natural superfood for energy and antioxidants.
- Spirulina—it has high levels of omega 3, great for immune function and detoxification.
- Protein powder—if you want to make the smoothie a little thicker and more filling, this is an option.
- Ginger—it is great for easing digestion and calming your stomach.
- Fresh mint leaves—mint adds a natural sweet flavor.

Step 2: Hydrate yourself.

Drink more water. None of us drinks enough water. Our bodies are made up of between 60 and 75 percent water. Buy a filter jug or filter for your faucet to filter out contaminants, and fill up a water bottle to carry with you everywhere. On average, men should drink about three liters (thirteen cups) a day and women about 2.2 liters (nine cups).

Step 3: Buy local produce or grow your own.

Find a co-op or farm delivery service near you. Sign up for the basic package to ensure you don't get overwhelmed and land up wasting produce. Each week, a box full of vegetables and fruit will magically arrive on your doorstep, giving you plenty of greens for your smoothies and sides. Alternatively, once a week, visit the local farmer's market. Buy your meat, cheese, and vegetables from farmers who are local to your area. That way, you know the food will be fresh. Typically, small farmers practice organic, animal-friendly farming, and you will be keeping local farmers in business.

If that is not in your budget, starting a vegetable garden is fun, rewarding, and inexpensive. Here are some tips to get you started:

- Look for heirloom seeds (typically sold online) to avoid GMO plants.
- Start the seedlings in trays in late winter/early spring before transplanting into the yard.
- Choose an area of your yard that receives at least six hours of sunlight a day, and turn the soil or build a box.
- Add some natural compost, like cow manure, and plant your food garden.

Once you start, you will be hooked. Watching those little vegetables grow is an amazing way to reconnect with the miracle of creation.

Step 4: Eat in rather than out.

Learn to cook simple dishes using fresh vegetables to ensure you are getting your daily quota.

When your veggie box arrives or your garden starts producing, take pleasure in venturing into new types of food. You can find recipes for anything online. My simple strategy is to look at what I have in my fridge and cupboard and then do a search using those terms to find a recipe that uses what I have. If I try to plan it the other way, it becomes too complicated with way too many ingredients I have to go buy. The secret to cooking is to keep it simple. Believe me, I didn't start cooking until two years ago. Now I find it an enjoyable, creative experience.

Step 5: Buy organic.

If it is financially viable, shop for your produce at a health-food store. You have to avoid genetically modified food completely. Tampering with how our food is created is against nature. And supplying people food that has been sprayed with toxic chemicals is unethical and dangerous. If you don't have a health-food store near you or can't afford it, then use your local grocery store but avoid the middle aisles of the grocery. Of course, you do have to venture in there once a month for toilet paper, spices, and other essentials, but for the rest of the month, stay on the edges of the store.

Supplement your vegetables from the organic section of the produce area, which can be found in most mainstream stores now. If you have to buy nonorganic, avoid the Environmental Working Group's (EWG) "Dirty Dozen Plus": apples, celery, cherry tomatoes, cucumbers, grapes, hot peppers, nectarines (imported), peaches, potatoes, spinach, strawberries, sweet bell peppers, kale/collard greens, and summer squash.

Foods that are least contaminated on EWG's Clean 15 list are: asparagus, avocados, cabbage, cantaloupe, sweet corn, eggplant, grapefruit, kiwi, mangos, mushrooms, onions, papayas, pineapples, sweet peas (frozen), and sweet potatoes.

Review whether they have any naturally raised meats.

Establish whether they have gluten-free products and learn how to recognize them. Most stores identify which products are gluten free or put them in one section of the store.

Select almond (if you are not allergic to nuts) or coconut milk. Soy milk can be problematic if you have a thyroid condition, as it mimics hormones.

Choose free-range eggs if your grocery has them; otherwise, purchase them at the farmer's market. They are more likely to be truly free-ranging hens. Or if you are feeling adventurous raise your own hens and get free eggs delivered in your backyard daily.

Look around to see if you can support other local businesses who may be supplying herbs or olive oil as opposed to purchasing the mass-produced.

I have come to accept the feeling of not knowing where I am going. And I have trained myself to love it. Because it is only when we are suspended in mid-air with no landing in sight, that we force our wings to unravel and alas begin our flight. And as we fly, we still may not know where we are going to. But the miracle is in the unfolding of the wings. You may not know where you're going, but you know that so long as you spread your wings, the winds will carry you.

—C. JoyBell C.

Stage 3 of Change

The Sapling

After the trial and error of stage 2, you should be starting to firm up the path of what change will look like for you. There are still gaps, but your desire for change is growing, which overrides the lingering resistance you may feel. You are feeling stronger and more resolved that the path is getting clearer.

But just when you think things might get easier, you encounter the barriers. This stage can be described as seeing glimpses of a path ahead through the signs and coincidences that the universe sends you to affirm you are heading in the right direction. Your excitement grows as you start on the journey, only to find it is cut short by the multiple barriers in the way.

You may curse and wonder why you ever attempted to change. It is important to recognize that these are not barriers but growth opportunities. They are a test of your strength of commitment and an opportunity to spiral higher.

By viewing them in a positive light, you can start processing what they are teaching you about yourself and your role in life. They also teach you about others and how to determine who fits into your life and who doesn't. And lastly, at the end of the conquering of a challenge, you emerge equipped with new skills and confidence you didn't have before. Don't let these barriers trip you up. Equip yourself with resources, coaches for support, or books to help you make sense of each learning you are being given.

One of the barriers may be your health. If you are struggling with ill health, low energy, food addictions, depression, or other signs of a life out of balance, you will have a hard time making progress. In the previous stage, you started to make changes to your diet, the results of which you should now be feeling. Food is your fuel for the journey, and you need energy-giving nutrients. You may still have health issues, which you can tackle now that you have a little more energy to devote to getting yourself optimally well. The reason you need a boost for this stage is because you may have to work really hard to figure out what is wrong with your body. I did, and for me, it took thirty years to finally figure out what was causing my health issues.

My health started to give me trouble in my teens, with hypoglycemic episodes stealing my body's energy. Experts tested me and offered up theories, but nobody could pin down what was going on. This pattern continued through my twenties when I added an autoimmune thyroid condition to my list of issues along with other weird neurological and stomach complaints. I also appeared to be allergic to three antibiotics. By that time, I had cut all sugar from my diet to try control the hypoglycemia. I also determined I was lactose intolerant, so bye-bye milk. But I could find nothing that was specific enough to know what was going on.

My thirties were an absolute health nightmare. I had mononucleosis and vertigo. I would get sick every month without knowing why. I was told in an offhand manner that I had IBS, and during a colonoscopy, they found precancerous polyps. I later contracted *Clostridium difficile* (*C. diff*) a serious bacterial infection that can cause death. They believed this was in reaction to an antibiotic allergy.

Having always wanted to be a mother I was devastated to find out I was infertile with no known cause. Grieving for the babies I would never have was a very raw and painful experience and never could I have imagined (as I found out later) that the infertility was related to the long-standing health issues I was having. The doctors weren't connecting the dots of my health crisis so I never thought to do the same.

My legs would get numb. I'd have pins and needles in my face and brain, which I couldn't fully explain without seeming crazy. I went to specialist after specialist and had test after test with no answers. By this time, I had determined that I was obviously meant to have been on the reject pile at conception and had somehow made it through with the cost of that entry ticket being living with a lifetime of ill health.

My health issues were still getting worse, and I finally figured out to cut gluten from my diet. Hallelujah! That made a huge difference and started me on a path to really looking at what I put in my mouth. But it seemed that even though I was getting healthier in what I ate, I was still struggling with my health. I started removing chemicals from our home. We had the ductwork replaced. I filtered my water, but things were still escalating downhill.

Finally, it all reached a crisis point. We went backpacking, and I was bitten by a tick that we only found two days later. I didn't think anything of it, not knowing what you can catch from ticks. When I got a severe allergic reaction to poison ivy, I went for a steroid shot, which suppressed my immune system. Things went crazy from there. My heart rate dropped to super-low levels. My thyroid levels were swinging up and down. I was chronically tired. I couldn't remember things. I couldn't understand what people were saying to me. I experienced panic attacks and anxiety over things that shouldn't have bothered me. I couldn't handle stress and had emotional outbursts which was unusual for me. But of course, because I believed I was flawed and doctors had never been able to tell me what was wrong, I just kept working at my stressful job and gave up getting tested and instead decided to try alternative remedies to deal with the symptoms.

Then one day, the wheels fell off. I couldn't get out of bed. I couldn't think straight. I couldn't perform simple acts like opening a jar of honey. My body was in a complete shutdown.

After having no luck with local doctors, I found an integrative medicine doctor, who was also Lyme literate, and she potentially saved my life because the next stage in cellular dysfunction would have been cancer. Thankfully she gave me the answers I had been searching thirty years for and while the diagnosis was horrible, I was incredibly happy to know what I had been dealing with for most of my life. Turns out I was bitten by two ticks when I was ten and had gotten sick, but in those days, they had no blood tests to tell what infections I had. Based on my history, my doctor suspected I was infected with Lyme disease in addition to the rickettsia I was diagnosed with at the time. My immune system had been keeping it in control, however with the most recent tick bite, the diseases went on the rampage. Chronic Lyme either manifests in the joints or the brain. Mine was neurological which means it crossed the blood brain barrier, a protective mechanism that typically keeps your brain safe. At some point in my life, I picked up two other bacteria, *Mycoplasma pneumoniae* and *Chlamydophila pneumoniae,* which start in your lungs but if untreated become systemic and move into your cells where they cause similar havoc to Lyme disease. Cells are the powerhouse where your mitochondria generate 90 percent of the energy needed to keep your body functioning. Keeping them healthy and free of invaders is critical to good health.

My immune system was in total disarray. The test for auto-immune activity was off the charts and in addition to the auto-immune thyroid disease (Hashimoto's thyroiditis), I also have another autoimmune disease called Sjogren's Syndrome. Scarily, I had been told in the past by an endocrinologist that the typical pattern was that once you had one autoimmune disease, you would keep getting more. I remember being horrified that nobody questioned why that was. Instead they just accepted it as a fact. Fortunately, with the positive Lyme test and the identification of the co-infections, I received the answer to what was causing my body to fight itself before I developed an autoimmune disease that permanently impacted my quality of life. The ones I have are manageable.

In addition, I tested positive for MTHFR, a common inherited genetic disorder that affects the efficacy of how your body functions. It explains why I was likely more susceptible to the failure of my body and finally gave me an answer to my family's poor health too. My father and both of his brothers died at an early age. One of the two types of MTHFR defects increases your risk of early heart disease.

After all the years of dysfunction my body was completely deficient in vitamins and minerals due to the undiagnosed gluten intolerance / celiac disease and the bacteria stealing nutrients from me. My ratio of good bacteria to bad was way out and I had to have a month's worth of supplements and probiotics before I was stable enough to start the antibiotic treatment. In the past I viewed antibiotics as the enemy, but in the right context they can work miracles, especially in the case of a bacterial invasion they are invaluable. Lyme spirochetes are very comfortable living in your body and have mechanisms they employ to avoid being eradicated even by the antibiotics. In order to fully process what was happening in my body, I had to become an amateur microbiologist, and delved deeply into the role bacteria play in disease.

Keeping the balance in your body is critical, and many people may be fighting an unseen enemy without realizing it. My advice to others who are struggling is this: if you have been living for years with weird symptoms and constant ailments it is highly likely that there is something else going on. The body is smart and knows how to maintain the balance naturally, however when it gets overwhelmed the internal crisis presents itself as seemingly unrelated symptoms. Write a health history and keep a health diary if you are concerned about your health. If it is a long list then get help as the downward spiral of chronic ill-health will continue to progress into a crisis change, unless you choose conscious change. Don't let doctors who are not willing to look at the big picture deter you from following your instinct about your health. You know your body best and if a doctor tries to give you a pill without giving you an answer to what is going on and why you have the symptoms, find another doctor.

Those were dark days, during which I wasn't sure I would ever get back to my old self. Most people don't understand what it is like to experience invisible illnesses, so you get little sympathy or support other than from those who get to directly live through it with you, those who have had it, or those who are educated about it. You never know if you will get better, and it feels like someone has stolen your life and left you in this deep, black hole. Eventually after eight months, I started to make progress on feeling physically better, and after twelve months, I began to get some mental energy and skills back. In all, it took 4 years before I was fully healed.

∿❦∿

You may run into struggles with relationships. When you start looking with fresh eyes at your life, it can often reveal the truth about what you have been putting up with that is no longer acceptable. You will have tough choices to make, as this is very much the selfish stage of your journey when it is absolutely all about you. All of your energy has to be conserved for your growth, your well-being, your blossoming into the most beautiful version of yourself.

After my divorce, I still carried my codependent nature with me, as I just didn't realize what I was doing. After continuing the cycle with a couple of really bad relationships where I was treated like I had no value, I realized that I had a choice: I could continue on with this cycle of abuse, or I could think about how those relationships started and figure out a different way to approach it. Every one of my prior relationships moved really fast with talk of marriage within a few months to get me hooked and then a period of retreat where I was left doubting myself and wondering what I had done wrong and what more I could do to make the person love me again.

Eventually, I recognized a pattern and started researching whether I kept attracting the same kind of man. Bingo! I found information on narcissistic personalities, and I had my answer. Narcissists are attracted to codependents. A codependent needs someone to latch on to, and a narcissist needs a fan club. But narcissists don't want just one adoring fan; they need many in their club. They keep attracting naïve women like me with their power and charm, get them to fall for them, and then keep them at a distance to avoid all the complications of a relationship.

After I understood my part in the pattern of unhappy relationships, I took a step back and decided I needed to be friends with someone first. I laid out my values for a healthy relationship in which partners are equals. The universe cheered and brought the perfect man into my life. Of course, it took me a little while to recognize it, but fortunately, he and the universe were patient. He pursued me in the good old-fashioned way. I chose to trust the universe to see where this relationship would go. And it blossomed into the most beautiful soul partnership, where we are equals. I am treated like gold and valued in a way I haven't experienced since childhood. As a team, we have faced challenge after challenge in our marriage and grown stronger in our love.

This was my third cycle of change.

❧

This is the sapling stage of the journey. You are soaring ever higher and spreading your wings through the branches you are extending into new space. You are stronger than the seedling in stage 2 and less likely to be defeated as you bend to the pressures exerted. However, know your tolerances and don't bend too far, or you will break. You will be pushed to the limit, but part of the learning in this stage is to know how to grow in the presence of pressure and stay tall.

You may cycle through this stage multiple times as you figure out what you really want and work through resolving long standing issues. Oftentimes, you start on multiple paths only to find that the path does not add up to your vision and you need to take a side path or return to the beginning and remap your route. This is not a sign of weakness; instead, it is a sign of knowing yourself well enough to recognize what will work for you and what won't. Be honest with yourself, as this is an important step to get right to avoid completely giving up and returning to stage 1.

The first wealth is health.
—Ralph Waldo Emerson

seven

Remedy Your Health

Modern medicine is about treating symptoms and regarding the body as a disconnected entity. To truly transform, you have to think of your body as an interconnected, energy-driven set of cells. Think of each cell as a puzzle piece in a giant puzzle called your body. Each piece needs the next piece to create the whole picture.

A wild body is one where your cells are functioning optimally. The mitochondria in your cells are your energy source. Energy is what drives every function in the body. If your cells are deficient or damaged, you will be functioning sub-optimally long before you notice symptoms or illness.

When cells start to malfunction because of food intolerances, environmental toxins, overdosing on unhealthy food, genetic defects, or bacterial invasion, the puzzle pieces start to lose their connections until eventually the beautiful picture that is your body starts to disintegrate and ultimately creates an environment where disease can take hold.

I subscribe to the school of thought that modern diseases are, at their root, caused by an imbalance in nature. We were created from bacteria, are surrounded by bacteria, and have a thriving colony of bacteria in our body. As with the universe, for all of these to function efficiently, there needs to be a balance. Many of the issues already covered in this book on toxins and unnatural food have created a complete breakdown in the efficient functioning of the bacteria within us.

I have experienced this firsthand and know that all the specialists and experts I saw could not figure out the truth of this. The reason why is that they were not looking at the complete picture but rather the individual pieces.

It is the same as divorcing us from the larger universe. The body has to be considered in the context of each part within, as well as all of the stressors outside. We are treating symptoms and not causes, and this has led to a multibillion dollar drug industry that thrives on our ill-health. Does this provide them with motivation to find the root cause? Highly unlikely, as that would be counter to their profit agenda. Healthy people do not need drugs to treat symptoms if they can fix the root cause.

It took me thirty years to regain my health, and I can only hope the lessons I learned will help you achieve it a whole lot quicker.

Wild Health Principles

You should sleep soundly through the night,
wake up energized, and be able to maintain
that feeling throughout the day.

You should not suffer from depression, anxiety, or lack
of interest and should have energy to live a full life.

You should not catch colds constantly, suffer from
allergies, or have other chronic undiagnosed ailments.

You should have a normal bowel movement every day.

The body is a whole system and needs to be diagnosed and
treated holistically with your input, as you know your body best.

Your Change Strategy

Step 1: Get tested.

These are the basic tests your doctor should run on you in addition to the standard ones already done at your annual physical to identify possible underlying health issues. You may or may not be showing symptoms or already experiencing health issues related to these. Regardless of your current state of health, it is important to know where you stand with these tests, as these disorders or diseases can be silently doing damage in the background, even without symptoms. If you are struggling with a slew of randomly weird health issues that you can't seem to resolve, these tests may hold answers for you.

- Vitamin B12 test

Vitamin B12 is a nutrient that helps keep the body's nerve and blood cells healthy and helps make DNA. If you are deficient, it can cause fatigue, rapid heart rate, stomach upset, and easy bruising.

- Vitamin D test

More is being learned about the valuable role that vitamin D plays. According to Dr. David Perlmutter, author of *Grain Brain*, vitamin D is not actually a vitamin but a fat-soluble steroid hormone that has far-reaching effects on the body and especially the brain.

- Gluten-sensitivity test

There are no accurate percentages on how many people are affected by gluten sensitivity, though one of the gluten-sensitivity testing labs, Enterolab, states that research shows that 30 percent of Americans have this issue, and 1 in 225 have celiac disease. The exact cause is unknown, but it is a growing issue and I recommend you try removing gluten from your diet, as the health benefits are evident more often than less. If you are experiencing headaches, brain fog, bloating, diarrhea, flu-like symptoms, hard to shake weight, bloating, and joint aches, you may be struggling with an intolerance to gluten.

- Thyroid test

Hypothyroidism (underactive) or hyperthyroidism (overactive) upsets the natural balance of chemical reactions in your body, causing multiple symptoms as your body struggles to cope. According to the American Thyroid Association, an estimated twenty million Americans have some form of thyroid disease and up to 60 percent of them are unaware of their condition.

- MTHFR

MTHFR is a gene that is thought to be defective for one in two people, according to Dr. Ben Lynch of MTHFR.net. This gene is responsible for making the MTHFR enzyme, and when the gene is defective, it affects how the enzyme functions. A defective gene may not cause any symptoms, but based on research reviewed by Dr. Lynch, it has been found to have implications in sixty-four conditions, including heart attacks, Alzheimer's, autism, depression, addictions, and type 1 diabetes. Every person should get tested for this to understand whether this is playing a role in his or her health conditions.

Step 2: Use high-quality supplements to address deficiencies.

Food is still the best source of vitamins however if you are not getting enough from your diet, you may need to supplement. Work with your doctor to determine the correct dosages and based on your test results whether you need additional supplementation beyond the basics. It can be overwhelming when you walk into a vitamin shop or the aisle at your drugstore so here are a few recommendations.

Some key things to look for:
- Are they natural? (Be aware though that the use of the term natural can be misleading and items like petroleum that is derived from a natural source can be labelled as natural)
- Are they GMO free?
- Are they gluten, dairy, soy free?
- How focused on cellular health are they? Some of my favorite health-boosting ingredients include turmeric,

olive oil extract, resveratrol, and green tea. A good multi-vitamin should have these rolled in to save you having to take a whole heap of additional supplements.

Here is a list of top supplements I would recommend based on common deficiencies. Be sure to adapt depending on what your testing indicates is needed:

1. Multivitamin/antioxidants:
   - to fight the free radicals caused by stress and environmental pollutants
   - may protect your body from cancer
   - to supplement the fresh fruits and vegetables you eat
2. Minerals
   - balance and regulate body chemistry
   - build teeth and bones
   - help efficiently metabolize nutrients
3. Omega 3 DHA (cod liver oil is one of the best sources for this)
   - heart health
   - joint health
   - reduced inflammation
   - brain health
4. Probiotic
   - digestive health
5. B12 (based on test results)
   - energy
   - decrease in fatigue
   - nerve health
   - heart health
6. Coenzyme Q10 (CoQ10)
   - heart health
   - may protect against cancers
   - supports digestion
7. Liver detox
   - liver health
8. Folate (based on test results)
   - production of red blood cells

- heart health
- brain health
9. Digestive enzymes
- supplements the digestive enzymes you get from raw food to support digestion
10. Magnesium (based on test results)
- stabilizes blood pressure / heart rhythm
- nerve health
- aids in the absorption of calcium
11. Turmeric

(Either add this to your cooking, or take it as a supplement. If taking a supplement, look for the active ingredient of turmeric, which is curcumin.)

- anti-inflammatory and antioxidant
- improves brain health
- may help in the prevention of Alzheimer's Disease
12. Zinc (based on test results)
- fights off colds
- helps with hormone production
- acts as an anti-inflammatory
- has antioxidant properties

Step 3: Ditch unnatural stimulants.

Rather than drinking coffee or soda through the day to keep yourself alert, consider using natural solutions to boost your energy. A few of my favorites for their antioxidant and natural energy-boosting properties are:

- goji berries
- baobab
- green tea

Step 4: Do an elimination diet.

To truly create dietary change, you have to eliminate the enemy from your fridge and pantry. Oftentimes, you may not be aware that you have a sensitivity to certain types of food, as inflammation can often be silent and symptomless in the early stages.

- Remove all gluten products. Substitute with gluten-free products.
- Remove all sugar-based food, including cookies, candy, condiments, and juices, sauces and salad dressings containing high-fructose corn syrup.
- Remove dairy products—milk, cheese, yogurt, and so on.
- Remove processed foods.
- Stop consuming alcohol and caffeine drinks.

Remove all of these products from your diet for one month. Document the following in your journal:

- Stomach reaction, e.g., less bloated, less constipated, less diarrhea
- Mucus: postnasal drip, sinus infections, allergy symptoms
- Mood: depression, irritability, stress reaction
- Energy: how do you feel first thing in the morning, midafternoon, and evening?
- Any other general symptoms

After one month, add items back using one of the eliminated food groups in each week of the second month. Record in your journal how you feel each time you add a food group back in. Your schedule will look like this:

Month 1: Eliminate all foods on the list.

Month 2

Week 1: Reintroduce gluten products.

Week 2: Remove gluten products; reintroduce dairy.

Week 3: Remove dairy and gluten; reintroduce sugar products.

Week 4: Remove dairy, gluten, and sugar; reintroduce processed foods.

Week 5: Remove dairy, gluten, sugar, and processed foods; reintroduce alcohol and caffeine drinks.

Take a look at your overall set of symptoms and how you felt, and identify where you see an improvement or reduction in your well-being. Any food groups causing an increase of symptoms should be eliminated completely, as you likely have a sensitivity that is contributing to your health issues.

Step 5: Switch to an integrative doctor.

Find an integrative doctor to help you with long-standing chronic health issues.

If you have cleaned up your diet and followed all of the above four steps and are not seeing an improvement, you should find an integrative or functional medicine doctor to do further testing.

The Consortium of Academic Health Centers for Integrative Medicine defines integrative medicine as:

> …the practice of medicine that reaffirms the importance of the relationship between practitioner and patient, focuses on the whole person, is informed by evidence, and makes use of all appropriate therapeutic approaches, healthcare professionals and disciplines to achieve optimal health and healing.

Simply put, integrative medical practitioners are doctors who balance the use of traditional medicine with the use of alternative practice in order to address an individual's health holistically. What to expect:

- Integrative medical practitioners will spend more time with you than traditional doctors. Typically, your first appointment will be one to two hours.
- They may not be covered by insurance. Check with your insurance company as to whether they are covered or you can use your health savings account; alternately save funds to work with one of these amazing professionals. You will never look at healthcare the same way again. And your endless visits to the doctor will cease.
- They will delve deep into root causes of issues rather than just treating symptoms.
- They will focus on mind, body, and spirit in recognition that disharmony in any area will affect all others.
- This will be a partnership between you and your practitioner. You will learn to tune in to your body better to allow you to give your doctor the full picture of what is happening.

But in every walk with Nature one
receives far more than he seeks.
—John Muir

eight

Retune Your Workout

Exercise should be fun. It should not feel like work. And it should be *free*. If it is not all of those things, then stop doing it. Wild beings need to be engaged with nature when doing exercise; otherwise, it will feel more like punishment than something to be enjoyed. Don't feel guilty if you hate exercising. Society dictates that you should be excited about running like a hamster on a wheel in a stale environment with a bunch of other smelly, sweaty people—and get to pay for the privilege of that experience! There is something wrong with this picture. Exercise should be natural. It should be an opportunity to continue to build your relationship with the natural world, whether it is as simple as a daily walk, a weekly hike, or a monthly row or kayak. When you remove the pressure from the experience and up the play factor, you will find that you have more motivation to get moving.

There are many benefits to exercising outdoors. According to a review of existing studies by a team at the Peninsula College of Medicine and Dentistry (published in the research journal *Environmental Science and Technology* on February 4, 2011), there are benefits to mental and physical well-being from taking exercise in the natural environment.

Eligible trials were those that compared the effects of outdoor exercise initiatives with those conducted indoors and which reported at least one physical or mental well-being outcome in adults or children.

The study found that most trials showed an improvement in mental well-being being outdoors. Compared with exercising indoors, exercising in natural environments was associated with:

- greater feelings of revitalization
- increased energy
- more positive engagement
- reduced tension, confusion, anger, and depression
- improved enjoyment and satisfaction with outdoor activity
- increased commitment to repeat the activity at a later date

Another study polled nearly two thousand active participants in the 2008 *Scottish Health Survey* and found that outdoor physical activity had a 50 percent greater positive effect on mental health than going to the gym. The researchers, from Glasgow University, found that walking, running, biking, and doing other outdoor activities in green space lowered stress.

The *International Journal of Obesity* reports on a study aimed at determining the link between time spent outdoors doing physical activity and the body mass index and weight of elementary-school children.

They found that the rates of being overweight of children who spent time outdoors were 27 to 41 percent lower. They came to the conclusion that outdoor activity might be an effective strategy for increasing physical activity and preventing increases in the number of overweight and obese children.

Being outdoors also prompts the body's own production of vitamin D, a critical ingredient your body needs to function effectively.

And the best benefit of all is that it is free, which will make your bank account feel healthier too.

Wild Workout Principles

Exercise should be fun.

Exercise should be mostly outside in nature.

Exercise should not be painful.

Exercise should not be about being better than someone else.

Exercise should not be in the pursuit of perfection.

Your Change Strategy

Step 1: Track your progress.
What you track improves.
Purchase a pedometer or exercise-tracking device. You can also download an app to your phone that will track your workouts. These do not need to cost a lot. Even a simple pedometer allows you to measure how much you are moving each day and set targets to improve your daily exercise quota.

Step 2: Make nature your gym.
Go outside. Right now. Smell the air. See the flowers. Hear the birds. Feel one with them. Start walking. Research local hiking or outdoor groups in your area. Look on Meetup, and sign up for one. Put your name down for a hike in the next week so you keep your resolve to do it.

Step 3: Join the backyard boot camp.
Increase the amount of backyard boot camp you do. Hand-pull weeds, for example. It is better for the environment, as you avoid using pesticides, and better for you, as you get to do squats without thinking about it. You can also dig holes, build fences and other physical exercise that gives you a good workout.

Step 4: Increase your incidental exercise.
Increase the amount of movement in your day. For example, park in the farthest parking spot at the grocery store and get the added benefit of a few more steps. Take the stairs rather than the elevator. Walk to the store rather than drive.

Step 5: Change up your workout.
Experiment with new forms of outdoor exercise to make sure that you continue to up the fun factor. Most meet-ups will have introductory sessions to allow you to try new and different activities. Fabulous workout routines include:

For warm weather and climates:

- wakeboarding or waterskiing
- kayaking
- backpacking
- sailing
- stand-up paddle boarding
- rowing

For cold weather and cooler climates:

- downhill/cross-country skiing
- snow hiking

Climb the mountains and get their good tidings. Nature's peace will flow into you as sunshine flows into trees. The winds will blow their own freshness into you and the storms their energy, while cares will drop off like autumn leaves.
—John Muir

nine

Reject Stress

Stress has become so integral to our lives that it is hard to divorce oneself from it. Adrenaline fuels our days, and when that starts to fail, sugar and caffeine keep the unnatural energy high. Coming down from this can be dramatic and often prompts people to avoid dealing with the reality of the addiction. You cannot feed your soul or your body in a naturally energizing way if stress is running and ruining your life. This change requires us to exercise tough love with ourselves and others, as we often feel we have no choice. You always have a choice, and if you tune in to your soul and body, they will tell you what they need.

There are two types of stress: positive, motivating stress and negative, energetically damaging stress. Positive, motivating stress is needed to launch a response to ensure our safety in a time of danger or for the body to launch an immune response.

The issue is when stress becomes chronic. This means that your response to stress never switches off, and you remain in a permanent state of fight or flight. I used to laughingly say that I had two speeds—150 percent or nothing. Now I know that is no joke. I was living on adrenaline which was necessary to keep my dysfunctional body functioning. But that was just creating the perfect storm, which eventually broke.

Stress can have positive and negative effects. Positive stress actually boosts your immune system. This is the kind of stress that occurs when you challenge yourself to try new things, stretching your mind and body. Chronic stress, on the other hand, suppresses your immune system.

Chronic stress is most often generated in the workplace. We have no means of controlling the demands that are placed on us, which means we live in a constant state of alert, ready to hit the next deadline or pull the proverbial rabbit out of the hat to ensure our continued employment. We are locked up in an unnatural environment for a minimum of eight hours a day, breathing stale air with our only exposure to nature a few unfortunate plants chosen for their ability to survive the sterile setting. Unless we opt to make changes to this part of our lives, this is an unfortunate side effect of the work environment. The best approach is to try to manage this using nature as your antidote to stress. According to recent research by Dr. Marc Berman and fellow researchers at the University of Michigan, taking a walk in a natural setting can boost performance on "tasks calling for sustained focus."

"Taking in the sights and sounds of nature appears to be especially beneficial for our minds." In fact, the researchers found that "performance on memory and attention tests improved by 20 percent after study subjects paused for a walk through an arboretum. When these people were sent on a break to stroll down a busy street in town, no cognitive boost was detected." Further research by Dr. Berman into what is known as attention restoration theory (ART) in 2012 showed that a walk in nature even had benefits for depression. The takeaway: if you work in an office, be sure to spend your lunch hour in the park.

Even living in a place that is removed from nature has a bearing on your levels of stress. A study conducted in 2011 found that growing up in a city or living in an urban environment carries a higher risk for mood disorders and anxiety. The international study, which involved Douglas Mental Health University Institute researcher Jens Pruessner, is the first to show that two distinct brain regions that regulate emotion and stress are affected by city living.

We all create our own stress by placing unrealistic demands on ourselves. We have to be the career superstar, the ideal parent, the attentive child, the super-toned athlete, the expert chef, and many more attributes that are fine in isolation but when combined are honestly not achievable. The pursuit of perfection can become a constant source of stress without us even realizing it.

We are also exposed to stress inflicted by others. Often, people in your life place emotional demands on you that are difficult to fulfill if you are already drained from job, health, environmental, and self-inflicted stress. When we feel like we are letting others down, we beat ourselves up and carry guilt around as a mark of our failure in that we weren't able to be all that others wanted us to be—which of course increases our stress yet again.

And lastly, we experience soul stress, which is a very difficult stress to identify but occurs when others tap into our energy and start feeding off it. Your soul is the wellspring from which your energy flows. A dry or energy-drained well will not sustain a vibrant body. Soul health is of equal importance in this journey as body or mind health. Time and attention need to be directed to identifying what your individual soul needs are and building a healthy, vibrant oasis that is protected from energy thieves. It is your choice whether you invest your soul energy in others. If you feel others are draining your soul oasis without your permission, then you will experience stress as you try to protect your most precious resource. People, thoughts, or memories that are soul-depleting need to be purged to allow the sweet and rejuvenating energy to flow.

Wild Balance Principles

You should not need caffeine and sugar to cope with your day.

If your job is creating negative stress, then
it is not the right job for you.

Make choices that lower your stress, not add to it.

Your finances should not be causing you stress.

Your relationships should be uplifting you and
feeding your growth, not pulling you down.

Your Change Strategy

Step 1: Make a value evaluation.

Reevaluate everyone and everything in your life, and determine what each is bringing to it—either negative or positive energy.

In order to fully understand others around you, it is important to understand a little about control dramas. We all have one, and it is important you spend time understanding your own and others' control dramas. This is by no means a complete list, but read through and see if you can identify which one/s may be at the root of how you interact with others.

I need:
- affection
- attention
- to tell others how it will be
- to feel superior
- to remain detached and be noncommittal
- to be introverted
- to be morally focused
- to be listened to
- to be worshipped
- to be needed
- to be perfect
- to be right
- to be popular

None of these are necessarily negative attributes. But if you don't take the time to understand this aspect of life, you will not gain the understanding that will help you be more empathetic yet removed. This is not a small step and can take a long period of time.

Start by looking at your family dynamic:
- What do you think is the underlying motive for your mother or father?
- How many of their traits did you take on?

- Did their or your siblings' behavior prompt a control drama in you that was in reaction to theirs?

Then look at your friend dynamics:

- What was it that drew you to each other?
- What do you like and dislike about your friends?

Then look at your own dynamic:

- What do you most often talk about?
- What makes your ego feel good?
- What are your expectations of others? List them, as they may give you a clue.
- What will you not tolerate in others or yourself?

If you have a friend you trust and have known a long time, ask him or her what he or she thinks, as friends will have perspectives you don't.

Write your thoughts in your change journal and continue to do so, as each time you learn something new, it adds on to the picture that you are gaining about yourself and others.

Step 2: Go easy on your adrenals.

Use natural energy boosters over coffee and sugar. My all-time favorite organic super-energy booster is baobab powder. I add it to my smoothies or cereal each morning. I only use a very small amount (about a quarter teaspoon) as it works so well that if you use too much you will have a sleepless night.

Baobab (pronounced bey-oh-bab) truly is a supercharged superfood. It is new to the market, but research has demonstrated it offers benefits to help control diabetes, reduce inflammation, lower LDL, improve gut bacteria, and boost energy, among others. Baobab surpasses all other superfoods and fruits. Here are the reasons why I take it every day and you may want to consider it too:

- It has antioxidants.
- It provides vitamin C.
- It is a source of dietary fiber.
- It has calcium.
- It is a source of magnesium, iron, and potassium.
- It is a natural, unprocessed, whole food.

- It is an organic, gluten-free, raw food that is sustainable and supports the local communities involved in harvesting the fruit.
- It tastes great. It has a very mild flavor, which can be described as a caramel pear with slight grapefruit taste. The flavor is not noticeable when added to smoothies or cereal, which makes it very easy to add it to your diet.

Step 3: Control your spending.

Get on board with the mantra "Frugal is the new wealthy."

- Jot down in your change journal what you value the most.
  - things versus experiences
  - toys versus travel
  - big house versus paid-off house
  - this season's fashion versus last season's
  - a new luxurious car versus a reliable paid for car
  - debt versus equity
  - stress versus freedom
- Decide what in your life is supporting those values and what is not.
- Recognize that stuff is not the answer to happiness.
- Analyze where you spend your money, and cut out the frivolous spending.
- Start purging things you don't need by giving them to charity or others who need them. Clutter creates chaos.

Step 4: Be imperfectly perfect.

Release the need to be perfect. You don't have to be perfect. You don't have to be living up to others' expectations constantly.

The Japanese have a term that I love called *wabi-sabi*. It is defined by *Wikipedia* as beauty that is imperfect, impermanent, and incomplete. It is the art of finding beauty in imperfection and simplicity in nature and accepting the natural cycle of growth, decay, and death. They view the ability to do more with less as profound and the removal of material weights a great achievement. *Wabi* stems from the root word *wa*, which means harmony, peace, tranquility, and balance. A person who is perfectly him- or herself and never desires to be anything else can be described as *wabi*.

Sabi means the bloom of time and refers to the natural progression. Age and the marks of age carry with them a dignity and grace that should be revered.

For us, this represents an ideal state where you can celebrate your quirks, wrinkles, and extra layers as marks of pride rather than shame, feeling content in the knowledge of your Zen-like state.

Take a leaf out of nature's book and recognize that creation is messy and imperfect. When the trees drop their leaves, do they stress about the mess they have made or that they have aged and lost their finery? No, they offer their leaves as a gift to protect the earth through the winter and revitalize the soil with nutrients to support new growth in the spring. Our goal should not be to sanitize and standardize life but to accept and celebrate the cycles of change that move us from youth to old age, that create chaos as children move from childhood to adulthood, that cause a mess when animals shed winter coats for summer.

We should admire ourselves for making meals, whether they are gourmet or not; for going for a walk, whether it is one mile or ten; for inviting friends into our homes for love and laughter, whether the house is clean or not.

We should always believe that if we are in tune with our wild side, then we are absolutely perfectly imperfect, as we are living in harmony with the larger universal orchestra.

Step 5: Banish the energy thieves.

Remove yourself from energy thieves. These are people who are struggling in their own lives but rather than embark on their own change journey, they decide to piggyback on yours. They feed off the energy that you are producing as you grow and flourish and yet don't channel anything back to you. You will know who an energy thief is in a number of ways:

- You will start to sense a heavy atmosphere when they are around.

- They will start to emulate what you do by "borrowing" your ideas and inspiration and passing it off as their own. Suddenly, you will feel like there is a carbon copy of you running around, which would be flattering if they gave you credit for being the inspiration. But no, energy thieves will never give you credit.
- They will betray your trust because ultimately they are not operating from a place of integrity but of greed. They feel no qualms about using and discarding you when they have had their fill of your energy.
- You will start to feel drained and confused about your sense of self because of the sabotaging that is happening.

Much as you may love them or care for them, you have got to put boundaries in place to preserve yourself from harm. You have an important journey to complete, and anything that is contrary to your personal mission is to be avoided. The more in tune you get with your wild nature, the more attractive you are to them. Your tree has grown in strength, but at this stage of growth, the dangers are often hidden. The growing tree may feel strong and invincible, yet inside its bark, a danger may be lurking that threatens its very survival. A termite is extremely small and may seem inconsequential in comparison to the oak, but the combined and continued force of several termites' actions can destroy all that the tree has worked so hard to create.

If you feel weird vibes from people you call friends or family, take note. That is your intuition warning you of an energy thief.

From a small seed a mighty trunk may grow.
—Aeschylus

Stage 4 of Change

The Tree

At this stage of the journey, you should feel like a twenty-foot-tall strong, towering tree. And that is the truth of it. You have created your very own beautiful Tree of Life that has its roots solidly in the ground and can reach up to the sky with no limits to growth.

The tree of life is a common motif in various world theologies, mythologies, and philosophies. It alludes to the interconnection of all life on our planet. The tree of life is a very powerful symbol to most ancient religions and is often viewed as the key to consciousness. Only by uniting body, mind, and spirit can you evolve into your wildly natural, spiritual self.

This book is about change, but not just physical change; spiritual change is a large part of the transformation to serve both you and the larger good. I have attempted through all the prior stages to connect the dots on how to use change to grow as a spiritual being. Having created the fertile ground of a content mind, healthy body, and energized soul, you can start immersing yourself in the expansion of your consciousness toward finding your larger purpose in life, the purpose you were placed on this earth to fulfill.

At this stage, you have conquered your intangible blockages—your fears, your resistance, and your lack of knowledge. You have also worked through your tangible barriers, like diet, health, and stress that tried to stop you from making the shift. You should have a bundle of learnings that you will need to sift through in this stage of change. This is where you gain the insight to see the big picture and the hindsight to learn from the past—to see where you came from, see the patterns that were holding you back, see the learnings you have gained on the journey, and see clearly the vision of where you are going.

This is the stage where your faith is rewarded and all the meaningless pieces in the change cycle come together into one meaningful picture. You are at peace with your decisions because your principles/values are in alignment with where you find yourself. You feel joy for overcoming your limitations to arrive at a place of contentment.

Your work is not done though. This stage of change is about the rapid growth of the tree as it climbs higher toward the sunshine and puts down deep roots into the earth. This is where you realize that you have accepted that change is a natural part of life and you start being proactive in how you implement change. You are more in touch with your intuition. You can read your own and others' energy so much more easily than you could before. And you start making plans for how to keep the positive energy flowing in your body and environment. You recognize what feeds your vision and purpose and what detracts from it.

At this point in your journey, you need to work on some of the ways you manifest your natural self in the community around you—the way you set an example for others about living in harmony with the environment, about working your passion, and about actively practicing giving more than you take from the world around you.

You may feel some confusion at this stage and question the motives of the people around you. You may also feel a little combative and fiercely defensive of your opinions and path. This is normal for this stage of your journey. You have redefined your moral outlook, and this may be in conflict with that of others who haven't. They may see your changes as threatening to their way of life and reject you for daring to go outside the norm.

It may be a sad realization that others are unable to support you in your journey. They are at different stages of their journey and have their own work to do to form a relationship (or not) with change. Don't let this deter you or derail you from your path. People enter and leave our lives constantly, depending on the role they have to play. Determine what they can teach you (either positive or negative), and don't try to hold on to people who are no longer serving your larger plan and purpose. So long as you are being the best person you know how to be, your conscience can be clear that the conflict is due to being in different places on the journey.

When I experienced this fourth cycle of change, I found that it forced me to stand behind my beliefs even if it made me unpopular. I struggled with internal turmoil, as I wanted to continue to make everyone around me happy. While being content is good, being complacent is not. To fully live my new beliefs and reality, I had to make a firm commitment to them. If someone was not treating another person right, I had to speak up. If someone was putting his or her health at risk, I had to speak up, even if it came across as unsolicited advice. And if someone tried to exert his or her negative energy over me, I had to put my boundaries up. These days, it is popular to be edgy or mean about others, using humor to make the negative comments appear funny. Competition, comparison, and crassness dominate over kindness, caring, and empathy.

You have to build your inner reserves to keep focused on the larger good and not cave in to societal pressure to conform to a lesser standard of integrity. It gets easier with time, and the more you set an example, the more you will notice others standing by their principles and following your lead.

❧☙

It is not to say that all change at this stage will be proactive and planned. As with a tree, there is the threat of catastrophic events like lightning and tornados that can destroy what has been created. During this stage, you have to build comfort in the belief that these events are part of the larger law of nature, that all things are created and all things die, and that there may be many more change cycles that will be beyond your control. However, the way you react to change will be very different to how you reacted to change in stage 1. You have a well of strength that will help sustain you through the difficult times, as you know that it is a cycle through which you will pass on your path to an awareness and connection to all things within the universe.

Nature is not a place to visit. It is home.
—Gary Snyder

ten

Restore Your Home

Eating healthy without living healthy is only half of the solution. We are surrounded by environmental toxins, mold, irritants, and chemicals that are not only poisoning us but our earth, which we need to sustain us. Our waters, fish, food, and earth are becoming contaminated. Conscious thinking about our actions combined with careful choices can support our health and our children having a healthy planet to live on. Oftentimes, we may feel like it is too expensive to live green, but the cost to our health should be included in our evaluation of whether a change is worth making. The evidence is constantly mounting as to how environmental toxins are stored in our body.

According to the website chemicalbodyburden.com:

> Scientists estimate that everyone alive today carries within her or his body at least seven hundred contaminants, most of which have not been well studied (Onstot et al.). This is true whether we live in a rural or isolated area, in the middle of a large city, or near an industrialized area. Because many chemicals have the ability to attach to dust particles, catch air and water currents, and travel far from where they are produced or used, the globe is bathed in a chemical soup. Our bodies have no alternative but to absorb these chemicals and sometimes store them for long periods of time. Wherever we are, we all live in a chemically contaminated neighborhood.

According to the Campaign for Safe Cosmetics, safecosmet-ics.org, one billion tons of phthalates are produced worldwide each year. Phthalates are a class of several different chemicals that have various uses in consumer products: they soften vinyl plastics and are responsible for the smell of new vinyl shower curtains; some are used in food packaging; and others are common components of fragrances in air fresheners, perfumes, detergents, cleaning products, and more. They're used in cosmetics to hold color and scents and have also been found in nail polish and treatments.

Phthalates are commonly found in human blood and urine samples. A study by the US Centers for Disease Control and Prevention showed that 100 percent of people tested had dibutyl phthalate (DBP) in their bodies.

We are surrounded by a toxic cocktail that is slowly poisoning our body. By making very simple changes, we can start to reverse the toxic overload that our systems have to process on a constant basis. Don't overwhelm yourself with thinking huge when it comes to changes within your home (I'm not suggesting you rush out and install solar panels); instead, try to modify the easy habits that are within your control and budget.

Living green means taking the environmental perspective into account in as many personal, residential, transportation, and workplace decisions as possible. The reasons for living green are abundant: there are clear and present threats to our environment and our planet that, if left unattended, could cause permanent damage to the world that our children will inherit. But one need not become discouraged or overwhelmed. For the truth is, even in the face of these enormous challenges, individuals, acting both together and on their own, can make a difference.

Making a commitment to living green involves recognizing that nearly every choice that you make from this point forward can have an impact on both you and the environment. After making this commitment, however, there remains one more step, one that is at the crux of instituting this change and having it be a habit that sticks. You have to follow up on this green commitment by changing your attitudes, behaviors, and practices so that they are more consistent with living in harmony with our environment.

Our behavior will serve as an example to others—our neighbors, our coworkers, our children, and many others unknown to us. If people see us acting in an environmentally responsible manner, then they are likely to be positively influenced to do the same. But if they see us acting in an environmentally damaging manner—especially if these actions contradict our words—then we will have a negative impact on others. And so it is important to remember this fact: once we, as individuals, make a green commitment, others will be watching us in order to make sure that our deeds match our words. And if they do, the combined power of the two will create a very powerful and positive effect for good.

Bear in mind that making the green commitment is not an all-or-nothing decision. The green commitment begins with a change of heart, of course—an explicit emotional and intellectual decision to live one's life in greater accord with the world around us. But beyond that, greener living is a step-by-step process—small steps gradually followed by larger ones.

Wild Home Principles

Your home should not be full of toxic chemicals that are
a danger to you, your children, and animals. Instead,
use natural cleaners, pesticides, and products.

Be conscious of your water and energy use and select products
and appliances that are environmentally and "you" friendly.

Practice a life of minimalism and low impact.

All body-care products should be natural.
Try to go without makeup.

Recycle, reuse, or repurpose everything possible.

Your Change Strategy

Step one: Question your why.

The very first and most critical change strategy is to stop and think about the why. So much of our behavior is unconscious and programmed to the point where we don't stop and think about why we are doing it. Maybe that is how our parents did it and we just followed in their footsteps. Or maybe you find it convenient or easy and haven't really examined why you are not able to commit to a different way.

Some questions to get you started thinking about this are:

- Why do I live in the size house I do?
- Why do I have empty rooms to house furniture?
- Why do I feel the need to replace my car every few years?
- Why do I need to wear makeup all the time?
- Why do I need the latest fashions?
- Why is driving five minutes to the shop better than walking?
- Why am I afraid to drink filtered water from the faucet, and why do I feel bottled water is better?
- Why do I need to have a television going in the background all the time?
- Why do I need to watch television every night?
- Why do my kids need to play video games and watch television to distract themselves?
- Why do I throw everything into the garbage?
- Why do I take a clean towel out of the cupboard every couple of days?
- Why is it a problem to feel a little hot or a little cold on occasion?
- Why do I buy goods that have traveled thousands of miles rather than items that are produced locally?

You may find, in examining your answers, that your reasons are not the most solid. If your motives are driven by the fact that it is easier, it makes you feel more socially acceptable, or you are not sure, you probably need to rethink your priorities. Most of us are not able to make the connection between the everyday actions we take and the larger global crisis. Part of rewilding your home and lifestyle involves letting go of your preconceived ideas of what a successful life looks like. Driving an old car does not define who you are, nor does having the largest house on the block or the most made-up, youngest-looking face. These ideas are marketing traps designed to get you to buy more in the thought that it makes you more socially successful. Abandon those thoughts. Be a rebel, and reject the idea that more equals success. The honest truth is that after the financial crises we have experienced, less equals success. Witness the growth of tiny houses and people who are debt free, living life on their terms, free to make choices that may appear harder outwardly but inwardly are the conduit to connecting with their wildly natural selves. Life is meant to be a little hard. If you try to easy it up, you are doing yourself a disservice. You will move less, you will expose yourself to unhealthy habits, and you will be tied to a life of materialism. Is this the trap you want to live in? If the answer is no, then start by making the following changes.

Step 2: Recognize the difference between wants and needs.

Want is a tricky one. It is the second cousin of why. The reason is that as you examine your why, you start to question your wants. A simple way to determine if you have a want or a need is this: "If I don't get the item, will I starve, die, be exposed to the elements, get sick, feel cold, or lose my means of income or transport?"

If the item does not fall into any of those categories, then you can be sure it is a want. While I am not proposing stripping your life down to the bare essentials, there are multiple layers of wants that can be trimmed down. The next layer of needs is about comfort. Ask yourself: "Will this make my life more functional, more enjoyable and less stressful?"

If the answer is yes, then ask yourself: "Will I add additional financial stress or go into debt by purchasing this?"

If the answer is yes, then don't do it.

If the answer is no, then congratulations, you are likely in the financial position to add creature comforts.

Finally, ask yourself: "In purchasing this item, am I having a positive or negative impact on the environment?"

This may take a little research, but I encourage you to trace the journey that your product has made to arrive in your store. You may be shocked at the impact on people and the environment that has occurred in order to provide you with gratification. Think too about how long you will be satisfied with the item before feeling like you need to upgrade. And when you trade up for a newer model, what happens to the product after you have finished with it? Is it recyclable or reusable, or will it just be dumped in a landfill?

Once you have a true sense of the overall cost of your wants, you are likely to gain new perspective that makes you question what and how often you buy consumable goods.

A green home is one that is large enough to fulfill your functional needs and is healthy in the air, water, and light quality and yet has a low impact on you and the environment.

Step 3: Recycle, repurpose, and reuse.

Do you have a recycling bin/service at your home, or is there a recycling center near you? If so, start looking at each item before you throw it in the trash and evaluate:

- Should it go in the recycle bin?
- Can it be returned to a manufacturer for reuse?
- Can it be donated to a nonprofit?
- Could I repurpose it for my own use?
- Can I put it in the garden as compost?
- Can it be reused for a different purpose?
- Is it really at the end of its life, or can someone else use it for longer?

Plastic accounts for 60 to 80 percent of marine litter. Take your reusable bags to the grocery store. Pressure stores to charge for bags, as is the trend in other countries. If you do have plastic bags, return them to a store that recycles them.

Step 4: Conserve.

1. Water

Water is a finite resource and one which we are all guilty of being wasteful with. The way I motivate myself to be better about my water usage is to imagine a day where we had no water or had water restrictions on a permanent basis. How much more careful would I be with this scenario in mind? This drives me to be conscious about the following areas:

- limiting the length of my showers
- installing low-flow toilets
- not running the water when brushing my teeth
- only running the dishwasher when full and not washing the plates before putting them in the dishwasher (many people view the dishwasher as the sanitizer and wash the plates before they go in).
- installing a rain barrel to capture water from the downspout to water the yard

2. Power

Energy use is our largest household expense and represents a large drain on the environment. Keep these practices in mind as you go about your daily life:

- Switch off and unplug appliances and chargers when you are not using them.
- Turn off your dishwasher's drying cycle, and allow the dishes to air-dry. Run the dishwasher only when full.
- Install a drying line (if your neighborhood allows it), and air-dry your clothes as opposed to using your dryer.
- Install fluorescent light bulbs.
- Clean and replace air filters once a month.
- In the spring and fall, switch off your heating/air and open the windows to enjoy nature's cooling. In winter,

set the thermostat to 68 degrees Fahrenheit when you are awake and 55 degrees Fahrenheit while you are asleep. In summer, set the thermostat to 78 degrees Fahrenheit when you are out of the house.

- On very hot days, keep the blinds closed during the hottest part of the day. On cold days, switch the routine and open the blinds during the warmest part of the day and close early in the evening to keep the warmth in.
- When it comes time to replace appliances, choose energy-efficient models. Fridge temperature should be between 38 and 42 degrees Fahrenheit. Freezer temperature should be between 0 and 5 degrees Fahrenheit.
- Ensure the sleep and hibernate mode on your computer are enabled to limit the energy consumed when you are not using it.
- Set the thermostat on your hot water heater to 120 degrees.
- Switch off the lights when you leave a room.

Step 5: Ban poisons that harm us and nature.

1. Cleaning / Personal Care / Cosmetics

Ditch any of these products that are not 100 percent natural. There really is no other way to say that. If you don't, you are poisoning yourself, as these products come in contact with your skin where they are absorbed daily. Additionally, you breathe in the harmful chemical fragrances.

Buy or make your own natural cleaning products. There are four key ingredients for natural cleaning products—white vinegar, lemon, baking soda, and hydrogen peroxide. If you want a lovely scent, you can add essential oils.

2. Sunscreen

Research done by Roberto Danovaro of the Polytechnic University of Marche in Italy and first reported by *National Geographic* in 2008 has shown in both lab conditions and field study that chemicals in sunscreen interfere with the algae that the coral feeds off by activating viruses that kill the algae and effectively starves the coral. The solution is to purchase sunscreen that has zinc oxide as the only ingredient, as that is a natural substance that does not harm the coral or you.

3. Insecticides

There are many ecofriendly pest control services now that use 100 percent natural methods. You can also make your own by using neem oil and essential oils of rosemary and lavender. Take one gallon of water, and add two tablespoons of neem oil and a half teaspoon of rosemary and lavender oils. Add to spray bottle.

4. Weed Killer

To kill weeds on driveways and pavers where you don't want them to grow back, a natural solution is to take a gallon of vinegar, two cups of Epsom salts, and a quarter cup of dish detergent. Nothing will grow in the spot after you spray so don't use on your soil where you want plants to grow.

In your flower beds, make sure to use mulch to cut down on the spread of unwanted weeds. And get a little extra exercise by hand-pulling them.

5. Bug Spray

I have never understood why people use DEET when it is such a toxic chemical for both us and the environment. If you are going to a malaria-endemic area, it may be worth the risk of using it to prevent malaria; however, for your average mosquito, citronella-, lemongrass-, or eucalyptus-based solutions are just as effective and are safer.

6. Cookware

Replace plastic food storage containers with glass ones to avoid chemicals leaching out if you reheat leftovers. If you have Teflon cookware, replace as you can with the healthier ceramic coated products.

His talent was as natural as the pattern that was made by the dust on a butterfly's wings. At one time he understood it no more than the butterfly did and he did not know when it was brushed or marred. Later he became conscious of his damaged wings and of their construction and he learned to think and could not fly anymore because the love of flight was gone and he could only remember when it had been effortless.

—Ernest Hemingway

eleven

Reignite Your Passion for Work

Once you have completed the previous steps, you are truly ready to decide if living your passion is a step you need to add to your life. It can carry risks, and you need to be invigorated, impassioned, emboldened, and healthy to achieve it.

This is truly the Everest of your journey, as it will take you very far out of your comfort zone. It can also introduce financial risk if you choose to start a new business or travel the world. But the reward of that view from your personal place of passion is immeasurable. The freedom of knowing you are self-sustaining financially as well as physically and spiritually is a heady feeling. The comfort you gain comes from a sense of fulfillment in laying your own trail and being true to your own beliefs.

Everyone is creative, no matter what you might say. And we all have unique gifts. It may not be immediately apparent to you what yours are, but if you continue the soul-searching and adventure-seeking habits, you will start to see yourself in a new light, a light that uncovers every nuance of yourself. Creativity can mean different things to different people. But whether it is creative cooking ideas or ways to train dogs, manage risk, or put your outfit together each day, these are your creative energies as much as the artist's or musician's. Knowing whether you are being true to your creative self is an important step of self-discovery. If you are not, think of ways to spend a little more time exploring and expanding your true gift.

I worked for a company for ten years, and whether it was a coincidence or not, they decided to make my department redundant after I fell ill. Not only did I lose my identity as a person through Lyme disease, I also lost my sense of identity as a contributing member of society.

I chose to view it as a kick in the pants from the universe, an opportunity to find my true calling and live a life of purpose. I started studying and learning about wellness and had a light-bulb moment when I realized that I could help people find wellness by using the exact skills I had learned in the corporate world—how to be a change agent and create successful change. Instead of helping people adjust to the challenges of new processes and systems, I could help them adjust to the challenges of life.

Journeying through this stage of the fourth change cycle was an incredible experience. I thought I had learned all I needed to learn, but being an entrepreneur unveils a new layer of learning. You will be challenged to examine every one of your bad habits as far as procrastination, applying yourself, and learning to be fully financially self-sufficient. It also opened up a portal to my past hurts that had defined some of my fears that self-sabotaged my progress.

At this stage of the change journey, it is acceptable to look backward for a short time, as you need to have a healthy outlook on money, success, responsibility, and accountability, if you are considering being an entrepreneur.

As your understanding of yourself is much greater, you should be able to navigate this retrospection without getting emotionally caught up in it. Stay neutral to the hurts, and analyze only as much as required to keep yourself growing. You may also rediscover career paths that you had considered in your past but were deterred from pursuing. Now is the time to dust off those old dreams and see how they fit in your change vision.

Each and every one of you has a journey that is just waiting for you to take. It won't be easy and will push you to your limits at times, but it is worth taking. You owe it to yourself and the universe to find your place of peace and purpose. You have a great story that is just waiting to be written. Don't look back one day and wonder what might have been.

Wild Work Principles

I love what I do and am living my passion.

I am excited to get to work and feel fulfilled by what I do.

I feel valued in my working contribution.

My work feeds a larger purpose.

I have balance between my home and work life.

Your Change Strategy

Step 1: Have an exit strategy.

Do not change your job if you don't have a strategy. Knee-jerk reactions to an unhappy working situation are not going to be the type of change that you are seeking.

All positive changes need planning, and a career change needs the most planning of any. Your livelihood is an integral part of your survival, and decisions regarding it should not be taken lightly.

A few strategies to consider for your plan:

1. Tag team.

If you have a partner, examine whether one of you can support the other while you explore a new career.

- Be honest and open when you discuss this, as you don't want repercussions or blame later if the partner still working feels taken advantage of.
- You will also need to examine your budget to see whether you can live on one salary without feeling like you are losing out.
- Start cutting out unnecessary expenses six months to a year before you decide to make the change.
- Ensure you have saved enough to carry you for the length of time you feel it will take to get your business going.
- Pay off all your short-term debt before thinking of making a change. That means all your loans, credit cards, and car loans. The exception is your mortgage. It makes life simpler if you only have one debt to be concerned about.
- Limit your use of credit cards.

My husband and I did this, and it worked really well. I continued working while he worked on the purchase of a firm. Later, he was able to do the same for me.

2. Do it dually.

Another option is to start your new career while keeping your day job. This can be very effective, as you don't expose yourself to any risk, can fund the start-up costs with your salary, and if it doesn't work, you can continue working while you figure out a new plan.

- Make sure your health is strong, and you have the energy to make this work. Adding more stress if you are already frazzled is not going to make you feel happier.
- This works better if it is an online business that can be run in the evenings and weekends. You don't want to be disloyal to your company by having your new endeavor infringe on your ability to do your job.

3. Study your way out.

A third option is to choose a course of study in a new line of work that you can complete part-time or online while working in your existing job. You may be fortunate, and your company might allow you to work flexible hours in order to facilitate your training, or you can use evening and weekend hours.

4. Be a part-timer.

If you really can't bear to stay and your health and financial affairs are in order, a final option is to leave and find a part-time job that will pay your bills. This will allow you enough time to work on your business or new career while still bringing in income. Part-time jobs typically carry less stress, so this option can be beneficial. Be sure you know whether you are willing to do a job that may be more manual and is definitely going to have less pay and authority than your previous role. You are making a change, and in order to realize the rewards, you need to be willing to make the necessary sacrifices with humility and dignity.

Step 2: Mine your passions; don't mirror others.

One of the hardest parts of creating a new career is figuring out which career you should be moving to. For some people, it is an easy decision, as they have a passion, people compliment them on their passion, and they recognize that people will pay for them to do it as a living.

For multi-passionate people, it is a lot harder. You are interested in so many things that you can fall into the habit of mirroring others' passions as you constantly seek that which will fulfill you.

The first step therefore is recognizing that your goal is to find your unique attributes and talents. If you find yourself copying others, then you need to consciously stop doing that and ask yourself the following questions:

1. What am I good at? What is it that people compliment me on and thank me for doing?

2. What am I passionate about? What is it that gives me a fizzle of excitement in my belly when I am thinking of doing it?

3. What will people pay me for? Where do I have a talent that will fill an existing need or pain point for others?

4. Where those three circles intersect is where you can find what your possible new career is.

Step 3: Try it to see if it fits.

Once you decide what you feel may be the ideal career for you, the first step should be to test out this idea. This may involve speaking with other entrepreneurs in the same field, volunteering with organizations serving the market you want to serve, undertaking a short course of study, or doing a part-time job in the industry. Sometimes what you think you want to do is not always the case, which you discover once you try it out. Committing too far down a course of action can be soul destroying if you discover that it does not "fit" you after all. Don't view this as a failure, it is merely experimentation to test the waters. You may have to try multiple avenues before you find the right fit for you.

Step 4: Test, test, test.

Before you commit huge amounts of money to a changed career or business, make use of resources out there that can help you test your idea. There are many free websites that, with a small amount of knowledge and skill, you can set up and see what kind of response you get to your idea. Don't invest huge amounts of money before you see whether it will actually sell. A great idea will not pay the bills.

Step 5: Create a network of fellow entrepreneurs and change makers.

It can be a scary venture going it alone. Suddenly, you no longer have the structure and support of an established organization. You are it. You are the IT person, the accountant, the marketer, the developer, the designer, the educator, and the salesperson. There is a lot to learn about being an entrepreneur, and having a tribe of fellow businesspeople is critical to your success. You will have days when you wonder what on earth you did. You will have days when you are down to your last cent and you pray the universe is listening. And you will have days when you are crying in a corner and beating yourself up about being a failure and wanting to quit. These are all normal reactions, and your tribe will help you vent and celebrate and provide a wealth of knowledge and guidance that you just can't find in books. Ultimately having done the planning, decided the idea, trialed and tested it, and created a tribe, all that is left is to start before you think you are ready.

The best way to find yourself is to lose yourself in the service of others.
—Ralph Waldo Emerson

twelve

Restore Others

After all the incredible milestones you have achieved in changing your life, it is time to think larger, to share the love and knowledge and go out there to help create change for others. Find a charity or nonprofit you can contribute time, money, ideas, or energy to. Be bold in stepping out with your own change-creating initiative.

Believe in your ability, and as Gandhi said, be the change you wish to see. Live it, breathe it, and infuse it in others every day. Feed the world with positive energy because the more you give, the more you get back. The law of attraction truly works. Be grateful for all that you are and everything that you have, project only your best self into the world, and I promise the universe will smile and lift you to places you never imagined you'd see.

Wild Giving Principles

I love to give to others with my time, interest, or investment.

Creating joy in others' lives makes me feel wealthy.

I give thanks for all that others give to me.

I will share what I have materially with others less fortunate and won't donate to nonprofits with large salaries and little impact.

I will get out there and see the reality of the world rather than wear blinkers to how others suffer.

Your Change Strategy

Step 1: Gift your love.

There are many ways to show your love for others, whether human or animal. There are many dogs in shelters looking for love through adoption or fostering. There are elderly in homes needy for affection, attention, and entertainment. And there are children who need the investment of a kind heart to give them the love they may be lacking.

Step 2: Gift your time.

Volunteer to help create a trail, pick up trash, or coach kids.

Start out your efforts with something small. Most towns have a group that goes to clean up local rivers and parks. Or just put gloves on and take a walk around your neighborhood collecting garbage. Recycle what you can.

Step 3: Gift your finances.

Loan twenty-five dollars to entrepreneurs on Kiva so that they can make their dreams a reality. Watch your new business investment grow at the same time as a new livelihood flourishes where none existed before your help.

Kiva has amazing success stories and has a fantastic feel-good factor, as you can see tangible proof of how you made a difference. Kiva has a 98 percent repayment rate.

Step 4: Take a voluntourism trip.

There are many amazing trips you can take that will open your eyes and shift your perspective. Rescue or relief organizations around the world rely on voluntourism to provide a steady stream of helpers and income from the fee you pay for your trip. You may only do menial work, but every little bit helps. You get to see a new country, experience the eye-opening that comes from a new culture, and know that your money will go a long way to supporting real change being driven by dedicated people.

Step 5: Rethink materialistic giving.

I am a retail rebel who totally rejects the idea that we need more stuff. I also believe that gift giving is more about the personal investment than the financial investment in the gift. A gift signifies that you took a little of your personality and injected it into finding or creating something to transfer your energy to another. I personally would rather not receive a gift than receive something that had no feeling behind it. Here are some ideas:

1. Give an experience.

Life is about magical moments, not about must-have things. When you give the gift of an experience, you are creating a memory that will last far longer than that gadget, which is fun for all of a month and then loses its luster. Some tips for getting this right:

- Choose to replicate an experience that you loved.
- Find a one-off experience related to the person's hobbies or interests.
- If money is tight, you can create the experience yourself. Print off a voucher that describes a day of activities you have planned. For the healthy, outdoorsy, arty friend, you could chauffeur her to a nearby artsy town to do a gallery crawl with lunch at the latest farm-to-table restaurant, after which you could go hiking.

2. Gift your help.

Offer to paint a friend's kitchen or help him or her plant a garden if his or her budget or time is tight. That will always be appreciated. Give the person a small, useful gift related to the service, for example a hammer, with a gift tag attached describing what service you are giving. You have to make sure to agree to a date and follow through on it for the gift to keep its meaning.

3. Make a gift.

This is more fun that it seems even if you are not crafty, as I am very definitely not. There are heaps of websites with ideas on how to make things, and it really gets the creative juices going in a way that marching through the malls does not. A favorite gift I received was when a friend gave me a glass cake plate with a cake on it. I honestly loved the cake more than the plate. Cultivating creativity is becoming a lost art. By changing your gift routine to making rather than buying, you are encouraging creativity to grow both within yourself and others.

4. Buy local.

I try never to step foot inside a huge mall if I can help it, and big-box stores often make me feel ill because of the negative energy in those spaces. But I love small local shops with character that offer unique items. A huge benefit is that you are supporting the small business owner who has to compete with the large stores.

5. Support a friend's business.

Entrepreneurship is flourishing and people trying to make a go of their business will love if you give gifts of their products or services. Sending my money their way feels way better than lining the pockets of mainstream retailers.

6. Buy gifts on etsy.com.

I love, love, love the artistic nature of Etsy, and browsing through the items is like a heady overdose of creativity for me. Take pleasure in seeing what others are creating, and matching up their goodies with people's personalities for gifts is a lot of fun.

7. Give something green.

A living plant is a wonderful gift that keeps on giving. Marry up the neediness of the plant with the person you are giving it to. Serious gardeners you can give finicky plants to, but for those without a green thumb, try a foolproof plant. I love cacti, as they look amazing and are so easy to look after. My signature plant is an African violet, as I feel like I am giving them a little bit of my home country, which makes the gift more personal. For outside plants, you could also give a gift voucher to a garden center. Pick a small business owner in the area, as they really need the business as opposed to large home-improvement shops. I was given a tree once and that made me cry, as it told me that person understood me at my core, which was the most meaningful part of the gift.

8. Give skills.

Purchase an adult education course, how-to book, or online course that helps someone grow in skills, knowledge, or personal development. Know the person's interests or needs to ensure it is a perfect fit.

9. Give the gift of giving.

Rethink meaningless spending that could be better directed elsewhere. A good example of this is the guest gifts at a wedding or goodie bags for kids. When I got married, it was just after the tsunami in Japan. After looking at all the meaningless junk, we opted instead to donate the money we would have spent to a tsunami fund a Japanese friend recommended that was local and on the ground.

Kids get enough candy and toys. Next time you have a party for your children, make a donation to an animal shelter or rescue service and give the kids photos of the animals they helped save. They may not understand why there is no candy, but you will be planting a seed of consciousness, which, if watered enough, will grow in each child.

Isn't it time to turn your heart into a temple of fire?
—Rumi

Stage 5 of Change

The Seed Sower

This is a beautiful stage where you are living and breathing your new natural reality. You start to see opportunities to create change around every corner and feel energized about the potential for making a difference. It is no longer good enough to think small and limit your possibilities; you feel driven to share what you have learned and help others to create change in their lives.

Building from your vision created in stage 4, your purpose is now starting to bubble through your consciousness from a place deep within your soul. You are developing the ability to create new seeds to sow, whether to grow another's life, a business for yourself, or a nonprofit or to take an adventure to keep evolving your own soul. As the tree releases its seeds to soar to new lands and plant hope in the ground, your new ability will create an energy whirlwind around you that gathers momentum without even trying. You derive great joy from the balance you have and feel a harmonious connection with all creatures and the universe. You are unable to resist being a voice, a leader, an evangelist for good, as it is a fire burning strongly within you. This is it, the place of beauty inside that works to create beauty outside. Follow your calling to be a teacher, coach, or guide to others; the world needs you.

Remember though that you are issuing very delicate seeds into the wind. They have fragile wings that enable them to float long distances but are easily damaged. Until you are strong in yourself, be careful of those who might damage your fragile and developing purpose. You are now so much more highly sensitive to others' thoughts, motives, and feelings that you will likely have to learn to continue to recognize those people who bring positive energy and those who are energy thieves or carry negative energy around with them. They can be very detrimental to your energy aura, so learn to shield yourself. Don't judge, but do guard against getting drawn in and losing all the incredible vitality you have earned through the journey you have taken. Don't be deterred from releasing your seeds of change to help others grow – the more seeds you release, the more the message will spread.

Everyone's wild purpose manifests differently and at different times. You may need to go through a few cycles of change before you fully feel the harmony of a wild life in balance. It doesn't happen overnight. It is an ongoing cycle of take a step, evaluate, meditate, decide if it is right, and then move forward or change direction.

You likely have had glimpses of your purpose as you traveled through the change cycle, and as your intuition develops, you will learn which pieces are important to your personal story. Learn to recognize coincidences as being mile markers from the universe. Every new person you meet, place you go, comment you hear, picture you see, or word that pops into your head may be a piece of your purpose. Jot all of these down in your change journal. You may not understand now what they mean, but as you continue creating magic, you will reach a point where you'll go, "Oh, that will fit perfectly."

I had always wanted to be an author. I studied for it, worked in publishing, and then found myself in the corporate world. However, when the timing was right, the universe sent me the opportunity to work on a book and my mother reminded me of my childhood dream of being an author. Click. Everything fell into place exactly as the universe planned.

Another goal I have held onto since leaving South Africa is to have a business that allows me to travel back there on a regular basis. While I love to travel and enjoy leading others on trips, I never realized that I have a talent for designing itineraries until others pointed it out to me. After exploring a few options for a career, my husband encouraged me to get into travel and I haven't looked back since. I absolutely love creating magical travel experiences for people. It was right there in front of me but I just couldn't see it. Bingo! A 20 year goal achieved.

The beauty of this stage is that you should start finding the path that is so perfectly you. While it may not be exactly what you planned or imagined when you started back in stage 1 of your change journey, it will turn out to be the manifestation of the essence of your wild self and the fulfilment of the purpose you were created for.

Once the story does start taking shape, you will quickly know when it is right. Your sense of intuition will be your guide. Stay strong with your faith in yourself and the universe, and keep drawing strength and energy from nature, the eternal source of power.

Now is the time to unite the soul and the world. Now is the time to see the sunlight dancing as one with the shadows.
—Rumi

Your New Chapter 1
Reseed with Your Purpose

If you have reached this stage of your change journey, you should be feeling a natural high from the incredible insights you have discovered about yourself and the world around you. Your wild soul should be fizzing with joy and energy drawn from the larger universal pool. Most people who take the journey of natural change feel elated that they have discovered the secrets of the universe and want to share this awareness with others but fear that they may not understand. You may still encounter resistance, but you are not likely to let that hold you back from sharing your joy in living a life that is meaningful and overflowing with an abundance of love, happiness, and soul direction. You are invincible now.

You may have to face a few last remnants from your past life that will try to cast a final shadow of doubt as to whether you are qualified enough, knowledgeable enough, or bold enough to be all that the universe wishes you to be. This is the final test of your will, and the easiest way to push past it is to be vulnerable. Keep your ego in check, and start to share your journey with others. Blog about it, speak about it to others struggling, or write it in a book, as it will be the final cathartic phase before you are truly released from the constraints of a life that didn't fit you into one that is like a second skin. When you open up to others who are still taking their journeys or considering whether to start, you make them feel more normal in their quirks and hang-ups. Having a relationship of trust, healing, and love with the world around you and with yourself is the ultimate goal of this journey we have taken together.

Everyone starts this journey at a time that is exactly right for him or her. Having read this book through once, you may need to go back and work through the chapters slowly, feeling confident in the process and the outcome. Often, the spark comes from seeing something in others that you want for yourself. Use that as your inspiration to light your own spark if you are yet to start your change journey.

If you worked through the change stages of the book as you read it, be proud in the knowledge that at this point, you have completed the journey and are now a fully-fledged Change Maker. You are, by your very nature, going to shake things up with your ideas and energy. Your enthusiasm for the very art of living is infectious, and without even trying, you will inspire and guide others.

Wild Leader Principles

Inspire by example. Live a wild, natural, and positive life.

Be kind and empathetic, as everyone is
fighting his or her own battles.

Practice integrity in everything you do. At the end
of the day, your character is all you have.

Keep your courage to continually push the envelope
of what is possible for you and others.

Feed your passion constantly.

Your Change Strategy

At this stage of the journey, I am confident that you have ideas bursting out of you and are already in the process of making them a reality. Here are a few additional ideas on how to continue manifesting your vision for change:

- Support organizations that are fighting to make natural change happen; they need funding and passionate warriors to move the cause forward.
- Lobby your government on critical changes that support our wild-living principles.
- Write a book on your burning passion, as the ripple effect can be very powerful.
- Work or volunteer for a nonprofit organization.

You are living and breathing wild principles, and there is no limit to where you can go. My greatest wish is to make this earth and all its creatures wild, free, and well. And I know, without a doubt, with your help, it is achievable. So…

Live well.
Live free.
Live wild.

I thank You God for this most amazing day: for the leaping greenly spirits of trees and a blue true dream or sky; and for everything which is natural which is infinite which is yes.
—e. e. cummings

References

Stage 1, Chapter 1

Kasser, Tim. *The High Price of Materialism.* Cambridge: Bradford Books, 2002.

The Spiritual Research Foundation. "Sattva, Raja, Tama," 2012. www.spiritualresearchfoundation.org.

Saade, Chris. *Second Wave Spirituality: Passion for Peace, Passion for Justice.* Berkeley: North Atlantic Books, 2014.

Stage 1, Chapter 2

BuddhaSasana, "Karma," www.budsas.org.

Free Dictionary, s.v., "dharma," www.freedictionary.com.

Meditation Oasis. Nature Meditations, 2006. www.meditationoasis.com.

Stage 1, Chapter 3

Howard, Pierce. *The Owner's Manual for the Brain: Everyday Applications from Mind Brain Research.* Bard Press; Managing Director, Center for Applied Cognitive Sciences, Charlotte, NC, 2006.

Li, Q. "Effect of Forest Bathing Trips on Human Immune Function." *Environmental Health Preventive Medicine* 15 no. 1 (2010):9–17.

Terman, Michael. "Controlled Trial of Naturalistic Dawn Simulation and Negative Air Ionization for Seasonal Affective Disorder." Columbia University, New York, 2006.

Stage 2, Chapter 4

Sinatra, Stephen. "Earthing." 2014. www.earthing.com.

Stage 2, Chapter 5

Dean W (August 1981). "Effect of sweating". JAMA 246 (6): 623.

Oosterveld FG, Rasker JJ, Floors M, et al. (January 2009). "Infrared sauna in patients with rheumatoid arthritis and ankylosing spondylitis. A pilot study showed good tolerance, short-term improvement of pain and stiffness, and a trend towards long-term beneficial effects". Clin. Rheumatol. 28 (1): 29–34

Stage 2, Chapter 6

"Dirty Dozen Plus TM: EWG's Shopper's Guide to Pesticides in Produce" and "Clean 15 TM: EWG's Shopper's Guide to Pesticides in Produce." www.ewg.org.

Stage 3, Chapter 7

Enterolab. www.enterolab.com.

Lynch, Ben. www.mthfr.com.

Perlmutter, David, MD. *Grain Brain.* New York: Little Brown and Company, 2013.

Stage 3, Chapter 8

Cleland, V., D. Crawford, L. A. Baur, C. Hume, A. Timperio, and J. Salmon. "A Prospective Examination of Children's Time Spent Outdoors, Objectively Measured Physical Activity and Overweight." Centre for Physical Activity and Nutrition Research, Deakin University, Australia, and Discipline of Paediatrics and Child Health, University of Sydney, Clinical School, The Children's Hospital at Westmead, Australia. *International Journal of Obesity* (October 2008).

Coon, J. Thompson, K. Boddy, K. Stein, R. Whear, J. Barton, and M. H. Depledge. "Does Participating in Physical Activity in Outdoor Natural Environments Have a Greater Effect on Physical and Mental Wellbeing than Physical Activity Indoors? A Systematic Review." PenCLAHRC, Peninsula College of Medicine and Dentistry, University of Exeter, United Kingdom in conjunction with European Centre for the Environment and Human Health, Peninsula College of Medicine and Dentistry, University of Exeter,

United Kingdom and Department of Biological Sciences, University of Essex, United Kingdom (February 2011).

Corbett, Joan, Lisa Given, Linsay Gray, Alastair Leyland, Andy MacGregor, Louise Marryat, Martine Miller, and Susan Reid. *The Scottish Health Survey 2008.* Scottish Centre for Social Research, Edinburgh, and MRC Social and Public Health Sciences Unit, Glasgow (September 2009).

Stage 3, Chapter 9

Berman, Marc and fellow researchers at the University of Michigan. Research paper, *Psychological Science*, 2008.

Berman, Marc. "Interacting with Nature Improves Cognition and Affect for Individuals with Depression" *Journal of Affective Disorders.* Baycrest's Rotman Research Institute in Toronto, with partners from the University of Michigan and Stanford University.

Pruessner, Jens. *Nature.* Douglas Mental Health University Institute, 2011.

Stage 4, Chapter 10

Campaign for Safe Cosmetics, "Phthalates," 2011. www.safe-cosmetics.org.

Onstot, J., R. Ayling, and J. Stanley. "Characterization of HRGC/MS Unidentified Peaks from the Analysis of Human Adipose Tissue. Volume 1: Technical Approach." Washington, DC: U.S. Environmental Protection Agency Office of Toxic Substances (560/6-87-002a), 1987.

Roberto Danovaro, Polytechnic University of Marche, Italy, *National Geographic*, 2008.